YOUR LEADERSHIP JOURNEY
LIVING & LEADING "IN AND ON PURPOSE"

BY GWEN WEBBER-MCLEOD
IN SISTERSHIP WITH SUSAN TALLIA BESAW

ISBN 978-1-957221-02-1
Clare Songbirds Publishing House
Your Leadership Journey© 2023 Gwen Webber-McLeod

designed by

Graphic Designer, Tauri Howard

Library of Congress Control Number: 2023937750

All Rights Reserved. Clare Songbirds Publishing House retains right to reprint.
Permission to reprint individual poems must be obtained from the author who owns the copyright.

Printed in the United States of America
FIRST EDITION

Clare Songbirds Publishing House
140 Cottage Street
Auburn, New York 13021
www.claresongbirdspub.com

TABLE OF CONTENTS

Acknowledgments
4 Cs Affirmation
The Leadership Journey Philosophy
Preface
How to Use This book

Section One: "Living in and On Purpose":
Defining Your Leadership Philosophy Introduction

ESSAYS:
The 4 Cs of Effective Leadership
You Get What You Are
Your Reputation Matters-Your Personal Brand
Leading Beyond Your Job Title

WORKSHEETS:
Developing a Personal Mission Statement
Developing a Personal Elevator Pitch

RESOURCE ESSAYS:
Faith-based Leadership
Family Over Everything

RESULT OF LEARNING

2

Section Two: "Clear Your Path": Acquiring
Fundamental Leadership Skills Introduction

ESSAYS:
Trust
Leading Through Change
Communications Styles
Feedback

WORKSHEETS:

Determining your Communications Style
Straight Talk/Necessary Conversation
Having Difficult Conversations

RESOURCE ESSAYS:

Quote from Eleanor Roosevelt
It's Personal
Nothing to Do but Decide
Leading Thru Grief

RESULTS OF LEARNING

3

Section Three: "Legacy Building": Inspiring
New Generations of Leaders Introduction

ESSAYS:

The Unexpected Leader ®
Unbought Leadership
Living One Life as a Leader
Legacy Building
Paying It Forward

WORKSHEETS:

Legacy Building Actions

RESOURCE ESSAYS:

Everyday Leadership
Influencing Others Through Mentoring
Work Hard, Play harder
Stay on Track

RESULTS OF LEARNING

Results of Learning Compilation Worksheet
(for all three sections)

"Goal Setting": Creating a Personal
Leadership Plan Introduction

WORKSHEETS:

Defining Elements of the Plan
Final Leadership Plan Pages

FINAL THOUGHTS

Gwen's Personal Favorites Reading List
Gwen Webber-McLeod Biography

Inspirational Poem: Before you continue your learning reflect for a moment on

AN AFFIRMATION FOR CONFIDENCE COMPETENCE, COURAGE, AND CALM

In quiet reflection to Live and Lead "In and On purpose..."

I desire to live in conscious pursuit of my purpose.
Let me have the confidence to follow my life plan.
Let me have competence as I use my personal and
*   professional skills to walk my path.*
Let me have the courage to stand
*   for what is right at home and work.*
Let me be calm to quiet my mind and soul,
*   and focus on my leadership call.*
I am thankful for the community of leaders.
I appreciate how we support each other as we make
decisions that positively impact those we serve.

-Gwen Webber-McLeod, President/CEO Gwen, Inc.

ACKNOWLEDGMENTS

I dedicate this book to my beautiful family lovingly known as "Team Webber-McLeod." I am forever grateful to my husband Tracy, children and grandchildren Ashley, Travis, King and Tristan. These amazing people are the wind beneath my great big bold wings. They make it possible for me to daily live my wildest personal and professional dreams. I am also blessed to be the daughter of the late Lt. Colonel Charles E. Webber and my mother Barbara Webber. As a little girl they instilled in me the philosophy that the world is mine for the taking. They provided every resource needed to ensure that I, along with my sisters Mysha, Kim and Terri, became the women God called us to be. Because of them I can. Because of them I am.

Thank you to my twin-spirit Susan Tallia Besaw who guided me through the process of writing this book. Our shared skills, divergent styles, wild conversation, hours of laughter made it possible for us to birth and deliver this book we hope inspires new generations of women leaders now and into the future.

Thanks to the Gwen, Inc. team and my advisors - Judi Dixon, Kathryn Adams, Caeresa Richardson, Michele Driscoll, Deb Bode, Kim Hooper and Elaine Buffington. The expertise provided to Gwen, Inc. by this talented team of women allows me to be courageous and not do anything crazy. Together we annually achieve our mission of inspiring leaders to achieve business goals by developing the competencies of confidence, competence, courage, and calm.

My ancestors are my ultimate entourage. I walk like I have 3000 ancestors behind me because I do. From enslaved women to my mother, I descend from generations of black women who leveraged confidence, competence, courage, and calm to overcome the unthinkable. These women had every reason to quit yet they didn't. They didn't because they could see me coming behind them. They knew if they just held on I would eventually arrive and pick up where they left off. This book is evidence that I did just that. I, Gwen Webber-McLeod, am their legacy in action. Your Leadership Journey: Living and Leading "In and on Purpose" is one of the many ways I am putting my legacy in action, I am historically obligated to do all I can when I can to ensure new generation of women leaders continue the tradition of changing the world for the better of all. As the name of my nonprofit You Can't Fail, Inc. indicates, I believe in the depths of my soul I can't fail because my history proves time and again I can't. I devote the rest of my life to making my historical sisters proud.

THE LEADERSHIP JOURNEY PHILOSOPHY

Becoming a leader is an ever-evolving journey, a way of life. It is a very personal journey filled with joy and challenge. Leadership is a calling, not only a profession, in your daily life, you must be intentional, preparing yourself with head, heart, and spirit to do the important work of leading.

You must be in constant pursuit of purpose, building your family and career around your definitions of purpose. Daily I am strategically focused on being in conscious pursuit of my purpose and leveraging this journey to the life I choose to live, and to inspire other women on the path to successful leadership.

As the President/CEO of Gwen, Inc. each day is spent helping leaders achieve professional and personal outcomes by focusing on the competencies of confidence, competence, courage, and calm. These competencies give leaders the cornerstones to building success, helping to achieve the purpose which defines your leadership.

If a woman desires to live "in and on" purpose she must begin this process by believing she is enough! Smart enough. Talented enough. Beautiful enough. Professional enough. Believing in yourself is what gives women the courage to consciously pursue their purpose.

Being a leader is A "total body" experience, a way of life you experience in both your professional and personal life. It is not for the weak of heart, but requires courage and determination, and support from many in your personal circle. Being a leader is an ever-evolving journey: defining your leadership philosophy, learning skills, building your legacy. It is all about focusing on following a personal leadership plan you create, and modify as you move through life and career. Being a leader is about you, who you are, how you inspire and relate to others, both personal and professional.

Women's lives are busy and filled with distractions, and may make them feel lost and purposeless, useless feelings which add no value to life. I encourage women in these situations to pursue purpose as a way to regain direction and personal value. You must daily "live in and on purpose", believing you have what it takes to be successful.

Here you are now, about to immerse yourself in this book about embarking on your leadership journey. This book is filled with facts, thoughts, and wisdom; I hope it inspires you to live your life in and on purpose, sparking your life success.

Let every word seep deep into your spirit. Breathe. Reflect. Be gentle with yourself. Trust yourself. Believe this is your time to lead.

Because the answer every leader seeks already lies within

PREFACE

My personal journey to leadership began in my early twenties when I was promoted to my first mid-level management position. My career expanded, and before entering my thirties I found myself the executive director of a major nonprofit organization. It was at this moment I began to pay attention to my leadership journey and the journeys of others.

There are many stereotypes about leadership. They leave emerging leaders thinking there is only one way of being a leader, often based on a male leadership model. Established leaders buy into the stereotype and wonder whether or not the way they lead is helping or hindering company success.

This awareness inspired the creation of my company Gwen, Inc. A private sector leadership development corporation based in Auburn, New York and serving clients nationally. I ask all clients why they were selected to lead in their organizations. They pause...then say, "to be honest, I was selected because I've been in the company for enough time to demonstrate I can do the task in the job description. I know how to manage. No one even asked if I could lead."

This experience is common to most leaders. I saw the opportunity to challenge the stereotype and offer services and programs to individual leaders and leadership teams focused on driving business outcomes by being their authentic selves. We do this work focused on our mission of helping leaders achieve business outcomes by focusing on the competencies of confidence, competence, courage, and calm. At Gwen, Inc. We see these as competencies, not attributes. Our most successful clients work at each competency until they are skillful in each area. This enables them to be strategic about developing philosophies, skills, and behaviors of effective leadership. Additionally, we see that the leaders we serve use these competencies to build a legacy of leadership that extends into new generations of leaders.

This book is written to help you the reader be thoughtful and strategic about your leadership development. It is based on a series of essays I wrote for my monthly column "The Leadership Journey," published monthly in *The Citizen*, Auburn NY.

Each essay is selected to spark reflection on what leadership means to you. Throughout the book, there are worksheets and leadership tips to inspire you to develop a strategic framework for leading based on your personal mission, vision, and values.

The final section provides you with an opportunity to craft your own personal leadership development plan, as a workable guide to your leadership success, supporting your ongoing growth as a leader. Ultimately, it is my hope this book starts you thinking about building a leadership legacy in such a way that you live and lead with head, heart, and spirit.

Enjoy this book. Use the contents to develop into an authentic leader known for delivering results. Remember, leadership is a way of life and what you work on here is relevant to all aspects of life. It is my hope the experience you create as a result of reading this book helps you live and lead in and on purpose.

HOW TO USE THIS BOOK

"Somebody somewhere is depending on you to do what you have been called to do"

With Your Leadership Journey: Living and Leading "in and on purpose" as your guide, begin your life-long journey through leadership, seeing this as your way of life, as organic to your personal development, as essential to who you are. As you read and work through this book, we encourage you to set aside time for each section, to fully understand and embrace the concepts and insights you learn. Once you begin an essay topic, make a pact with yourself not to accept interruptions until you have finished the topic, and made any notes.

THE FIRST THREE SECTIONS

SECTION ONE:
"Living In and On Purpose":
Defining Your Leadership Philosophy

SECTION TWO:
"Clear Your Path":
Acquiring Fundamental Leadership Skills

SECTION THREE:
"Legacy Building":
Inspiring New Generations of Leaders

All give you real-life essays, specific worksheets, inspiring reflections, and the opportunity to journal your reactions to the section topic, providing you with the building blocks to define your personal leadership and skills.

Each chapter begins with an Introduction, introducing you to the concepts and skills to be reviewed, providing you with an overview of the content and usefulness of each essay, directions, and outcomes for each worksheet, and resource essays to consider as they may affect your personal leadership development.

ESSAY TOPICS

follow, based on Gwen's real-life observations about developing leadership. Be thoughtful as you read each essay, relating to your own experiences, reflecting and beginning to internalize your learning. Make notes, ask questions of yourself, and others, to fully integrate your thinking. After each article, writing space is provided for you to journal your reactions, and organize your comments, concerns, and questions about each essay.

SUBJECT WORKSHEETS

help you clarify the knowledge you gain, creating documents as your own personal resources, real tools to use as you deal with leadership and life challenges.

are reflective of the topics in each section, and are related to our "heart concerns." These essays are topics that frequently surface during discussions and seminars related to the central idea of each session, and you may find them helpful.

which leads you to consider the results of your learning helps center your new knowledge, giving you encouragement, and comfort, while working through the realities of leadership challenges. These reflections lead you to identify the concrete results of learning from each section, give you an opportunity for personal reflection.

RESULTS OF LEARNING

at the conclusion of each section a task is presented to you:
"As a result of studying this section, I will…"

You will find yourself confronted by a blank page. Use the space to specifically write down how your behavior will change after studying the section or to identify a very specific action you will take as a result of your learning. During your reading you may also have identified a nagging concern, a situation or question, write it down also. As you move through each section, you may find these questions and concerns may solve themselves with more knowledge. You will also have the opportunity to prepare a final compilation of these items before beginning your "Personal Leadership Plan" as they will affect your thinking.

At the conclusion of section three, a **Results of Learning Compilation** appears; use this page to compile the lists you have made from each learning section for behavior changes, actions taken, and active concerns and situations. This gives you an opportunity to review your real-life progress, and identify issues for inclusion in your **Personal Leadership Plan.**

SECTION FOUR:
Your Leadership Journey:
"Living and Leading "in and on purpose"

culminates in Section Four, **"Goal Setting": Creating a Personal Leadership Plan** which builds on learning from the prior sections. Using the lessons learned about yourself and your journey through leadership development, you will create your **Personal Leadership Plan**, a specific, workable guide you can refer to over and over, for the inspiration and skills to ensure your success. There is power in writing down your plan, it enables you to move from where you are on your leadership path, to become the leader you aspire to be. As you envision the leader you want to be, you now have a living tool to create your authentic self as a leader.

A short reading list of Gwen's personal favorites for leadership development is included as a further resource for your leadership development.

INTRODUCTION TO SECTION ONE
LIVING IN AND ON PURPOSE: DEFINING YOUR LEADERSHIP PHILOSOPHY

Defining your leadership philosophy is the first step in becoming an effective leader. **You "are what you think" in leadership.** What you think about being a leader informs everything you do and determines if others will follow you. The essays in this chapter provide insight into this essential first step in becoming a leader, urging you to think, consider, and discover your personal philosophies. Understanding your leadership philosophy is a way to be in conscious pursuit of your purpose; fully understanding who you are is at the core of being an effective leader. As you read each article, remember to use the space provided to make notes, ask questions of yourself, write down your concerns.

ESSAYS:

THE 4 Cs OF EFFECTIVE LEADERSHIP
A leadership model which promotes competence, confidence, courage, and calm as cornerstones to leadership success.

YOU GET WHAT YOU ARE
Discusses the direct connection between what you think and believe, how you act, and your leadership success.

YOUR REPUTATION MATTERS IT'S YOUR PERSONAL BRAND
Having a great reputation cements your personal brand for leadership success.

LEADING BEYOND YOUR JOB TITLE
Provides insights which help you define who you are as a leader, and what leading means to you.

WORKSHEETS:

DEVELOPING A PERSONAL MISSION STATEMENT
Your leadership philosophy should be developed based on your personal mission statement. This worksheet will be a resource as you work towards the goal of creating a personal leadership plan in section four of the book.

DEVELOPING A PERSONAL BRAND/ELEVATOR PITCH
This worksheet gives you step-by-step instructions for discovering the elements of your personal brand and developing them into your personal elevator pitch.

RESOURCE ARTICLES:

FAITH-BASED LEADERSHIP
A leadership model which promotes competence, confidence, courage, and calm as cornerstones to leadership success.

FAMILY OVER EVERYTHING
Discusses the direct connection between what you think and believe, how you act, and your leadership success.

INSPIRATIONAL POEM:
"Ready to Unfold" by Mona Lake Jones

RESULTS OF LEARNING:
Use the inspirational poem to help you focus on how your behavior will change as a result of working in this section. Write down specific actions you will take, any concerns or situations hindering your path to success.

THE 4 Cs OF EFFECTIVE LEADERSHIP

CONFIDENT, COMPETENT, COURAGEOUS, AND CALM

WHY DO YOU NEED THE 4 Cs ?

Personal and organizational effectiveness can be increased by focusing leaders on developing the 4 Cs: confidence, competence, courage, and calm. These competencies help leaders remain open to evolving with the changing times. Leaders themselves constantly change, any leader who thinks they are done evolving is DONE! Allow ideas about leadership to evolve with the changing needs of your work environment. Doing so will enhance the quality of your work and add value to your experiences as a successful leader.

CONFIDENCE

is an anchoring leadership competency that serves as a "springboard" for the development of the other Cs. Developing personal confidence is primary for career success and leads to other types of confidence that contribute to business success. When leaders develop strong strategic plans, they increase organizational confidence by providing specific focus and strategies for achieving business goals. Gaining and sustaining the confidence of internal and external stakeholders adds value to leadership efforts. The continual assessment of employee confidence in leaders helps build organizational culture. These additional forms of confidence position leaders to conduct good business on behalf of organizations and companies.

COMPETENCE

includes skills leaders develop to perform in the workplace. Today's business environment demands competence in new skill areas, which directly connects to building operational capacity in all industries. Nonprofit leaders are particularly challenged because current trends mandate they function more like private sector counterparts. Many leaders recognize current skills are not sufficient to ensure the long-term viability of the organization. Our competence building work takes on an organization development approach, emphasizing skills such as data-driven decision making, strategic critical thinking, sustaining market share, dealing with competition, sophisticated fiscal analysis, and strategic staffing and hiring.

Competence in these areas is a determinant of individual leadership success and the overall success of an organization or company. But technical competence is not enough, a successful leader must build and sustain high-trust relationships. There is a direct correlation between a highly trusted leader and driving successful outcomes, indeed, they are irrevocably linked.

COURAGE

may be the most important leadership competency. Many clients describe themselves as leading in extraordinary times. Having courage is no longer optional, it is an absolute necessity. Leaders report the need to courageously speak truth to power. Difficult situations can't linger and must be dealt with expeditiously and with great courage. Fiscal courage is necessary to align reduced resources into budgets that truly fund what is needed to sustain an organization. Effective leaders muster the courage to stop doing what is no longer relevant and promote bold and courageous visions for the future of the organization.

CALM

like confidence, is an anchoring competency in effective leadership. The well-known quote, "Peace. It does not mean to be in a place where there is no noise, trouble, or hard work. It means to be in the midst of those things and still be calm in your heart," speaks to the specific form of calm we see in talented leaders. Effective leaders infuse the workplace with calm decision making, working with employees to create workplace environments that encourage thoughtful consideration of important matters. Factors that disrupt calmness are quickly confronted. The goal is to help employees remain calmly productive even in the midst of noise and challenge that comes with hard work.

YOU GET WHAT YOU ARE

IS WORD/DEED ALIGNMENT EVIDENT IN YOUR LEADERSHIP?

I have the opportunity to work with established and emerging leaders countrywide. Leaders have the tremendous task of setting-up businesses and organizations for success, positioning for good community partnering, and keeping employees inspired so they show up every day with the energy to achieve goals. Wow! This is a huge leadership responsibility. How does one organize herself to handle the many exciting and challenging tasks of leading for success?

Believe you have all you need

It has been my experience that leadership success begins with a willingness to recognize that in your work you will get what you are. My observation is that most successful leaders are highly aware of word/deed alignment, and understand the connection between values, deeds, actions and earning respect as a leader. There is a direct connection between what you think, what you believe, how you act, and the success or lack of success you will experience in your leadership career. People get their cues on how to respond to you directly from you. People hear what you say, but only believe what they see you do; it is essential that you "walk your talk." There should be visible evidence that your leadership makes a difference.

You inspire people and they want to follow where you lead.

- **IF YOU WANT YOUR LEADERSHIP TO BE SUCCESSFUL, YOU MUST THINK, BELIEVE, AND ACT IN WAYS TO MAKE YOU SUCCESSFUL.**

- **IF YOU WANT TO BE KNOWN AS A GOOD COMMUNITY PARTNER, YOU MUST THINK, BELIEVE, AND ACT IN WAYS THAT LEAD TO GOOD COMMUNITY PARTNERSHIPS.**

- **IF YOU WANT OTHERS TO FOLLOW YOU, TO BE PRODUCTIVE AND LOYAL, YOU MUST THINK, BELIEVE, AND ACT IN WAYS THAT LET THEM KNOW THAT THIS IS WHAT YOU WANT FROM THEM.**

As you continue your leadership journey, I inspire you to pay close attention to the alignment of your words, deeds, actions, and results. These things together create "energy" that is applied to the development of leadership and business strategies. This energy allows you to create respectful workplace environments encouraging employees to do their best to help achieve goals. If you want to be a successful leader, you must align all these elements.

What you put out in the process of being a leader is what you will get in return.

You will get what you are.

SPACE FOR REFLECTION

YOUR REPUTATION MATTERS

IT'S YOUR PERSONAL BRAND

When I decided to incorporate a company, I turned to a master brander. We discussed how to develop a brand that would set my business apart in the marketplace. She told me: "Gwen, you are your business. Why do you think people choose to do business with you over others who do the same work in our region? How would you describe your personal brand?" The questions made me ponder the significance of leaders developing a personal brand.

A personal brand is another way to think about reputation. Having a great reputation is important for those interested in being effective leaders. Turning your reputation into a brand requires you to consciously monitor the interaction between who you are, what you do, your values and how people react to you. The combination of these factors, over time, cements your reputation into a personal brand. I've learned to think of a positive personal brand as a set of qualities and characteristics a leader desires to consistently be known for at work, home and in the community.

Leaders often believe they can't proactively affect people's perceptions of their personal brand. I believe leaders can and should pro-actively affect this aspect of their professional lives. If you don't, others will do it for you and it may not be the best representation of you.

Leaders can take specific actions to develop a positive reputation and personal brand:

- **DETERMINE THE QUALITIES, CHARACTERISTICS, AND VALUES YOU WANT TO BE KNOWN FOR, SUCH AS DEPENDABILITY, HONESTY, YOUR ATTITUDE TOWARD WORK**

- **COMMIT TO LIVING THESE CONSISTENTLY AS YOU LEAD**

ATTITUDE

What is your attitude? Is it working for you?

HONESTY

Do you do what you say you will do?

DEPENDABILITY

Can people rely on you?

Translate your qualities, characteristics and values into a personal mission statement, and an elevator speech. Both are great tools for managing your personal brand. They are resources that help leaders focus on the qualities and characteristics of their brand, holding you accountable to you.

We all know a leader who has a negative reputation. Are they effective? Are they viewed as having integrity? Are others willing to follow them? The value of a positive reputation, a personal brand is documented in leadership research over and over again: a positive personal brand adds significant value to one's effectiveness as a leader. I encourage leaders to think of themselves as "You, Inc." Spend time developing and managing your reputation, your personal brand, for your success is directly connected to these perceptions.

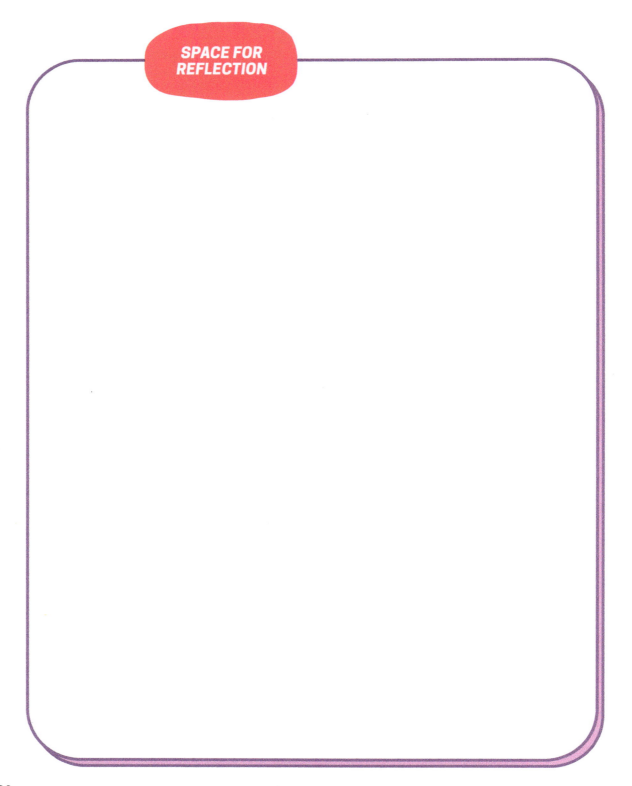
SPACE FOR REFLECTION

LEADING BEYOND YOUR JOB TITLE

IF YOU WERE STRIPPED OF YOUR TITLE WOULD YOUR EMPLOYEES, FAMILY, AND FRIENDS STILL FOLLOW YOU?

IF YOU WERE STRIPPED OF YOUR TITLE WOULD YOUR EMPLOYEES, FAMILY, AND FRIENDS STILL FOLLOW YOU?

I frequently ask clients this question during executive coaching sessions, encouraging leaders to think about the impact job titles have on their lives. Many leaders assume people follow them because of the position they hold. Some believe job titles give them leverage when it comes to office politics and the power to reward and punish. There is an element of truth to this, but effective leadership is about much more than a job title, and it should be.

As a leader, it is important to understand why people choose to follow you. It is equally important to understand why they won't. It is not a given that your title and the power that comes with it automatically motivates someone to follow your lead. People decide whether or not to follow a leader based on a number of factors. The "leader-follower" relationship is more complex than it appears on the surface. It is important to understand the relationship between how people perceive and feel about leaders and their willingness to follow. For example, employees comply with titles but are committed to follow and respect leaders who lead beyond their title.

These leaders view job titles as:

1 A resource for professional growth

2 Leverage for opportunities for team success.

3 A resource in building a legacy of leadership that lasts beyond their time in a position

As you think about pursuing your next job title, these tips will help clarify your thinking. It is important to reflect on why you want the title. I coach too many leaders who simply chase job titles without fully considering the ramifications of making a professional move. What is motivating your desire to have a new job title? If the answer is only money, rethink taking the title. Go into a period of discovery about your new opportunity. Make sure you fully understand expectations and be clear about what is truly in it for you.

DOES THE NEW TITLE HELP FINANCIALLY?

DOES THE NEW TITLE ALLOW YOU TO LIVE WITHIN YOUR VALUES?

DOES THE NEW TITLE ENABLE YOU TO BE THE SPOUSE OR PARENT YOU DESIRE TO BE?

New job titles impact more than day-to-day tasks. They impact every aspect of your life. Think about this as you position yourself to make your next professional move.

New job titles create opportunities to build a legacy of leadership. As you consider a new title think about how it enables you to help others.

As you evolve and seek new titles you just might learn leadership is not only about you. It is also about those you help along the way. In fact, when I speak with successful leaders, helping others is the primary reason they lead. Leaders often find their purpose as they progress from one job title to the next.

Your job title defines the tasks and authority you have at work. The time you spend in a certain position is finite, but the impact of leveraging your title to achieve business outcomes, develop people and improve the community lasts a lifetime.

IF YOU WERE STRIPPED OF YOUR TITLE WOULD YOUR EMPLOYEES, FAMILY, AND FRIENDS STILL FOLLOW YOU?

The answer is "yes" if you are intentional about designing a career that utilizes your job title to bring your best self to these various groups of people who follow you.

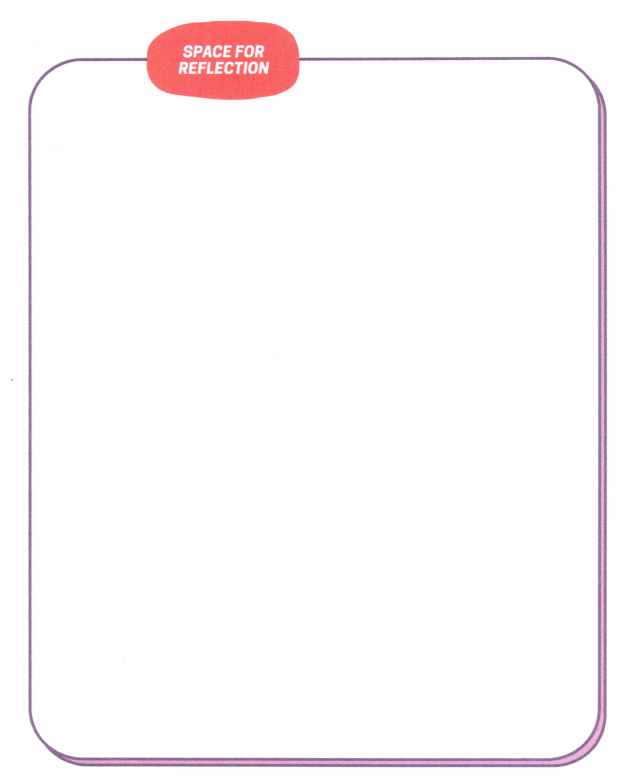

WHAT IS A PERSONAL MISSION STATEMENT AND WHY DO YOU NEED IT?

1. Read the introduction
2. Review sample mission statements provided here
3. Consider sampling statements on Google
4. Heed the tips provided for writing
5. Identify the resources available to you for support
6. Answer the questions provided to develop the statement
7. Consolidate your answers into a personal Mission Statement

INTRODUCTION:

A personal mission statement becomes a guiding light, an anchor of clarity that keeps you true to yourself when the winds of life-pressure blow through. It defines who you are, and what is important to you, giving you a foundation to stand on in your personal and professional life. It will help you clearly define what a woman will or will not tolerate in her life and set boundaries. In a world where it is easy to be blown around like a windsock with the day-to-day challenges of life, it helps to have something that grounds you. A Personal Mission Statement is a powerful resource in helping women live with confidence, competence, courage, and calm.

"To be a confident, competent, courageous, and calm woman leader, wife, mother, and activist whose legacy of leadership inspires other leaders, especially women of color, you have to believe it is possible to better the world by simply existing and living one's wildest dreams."

-Gwen Webber-McLeod

TIPS TO CONSIDER WHILE WRITING THE STATEMENT:

BE QUIET

BRAINSTORM

DON'T CENSOR YOURSELF

CONNECT YOUR IDEAS

DRAFT THE STATEMENT

USE SUB-STATEMENTS

REVISE THE STATEMENT

TEST IT OUT ON OTHERS

OWN THE STATEMENT

PERSONAL MISSION STATEMENT RESOURCES

What will help me write this statement?

What could hinder me from completing the statement?

What specific actions can I take to help me complete the statement?

Are there people who can help me?

What dates can I commit to?

start date:
complete date:

What is important to me?

When do I feel most connected to myself?

How do I want to relate to family and friends?

What are my strengths?

What do I want to be known for by my family, coworkers, community?

What do I value (relationships, faith, honesty, success)?

What things won't I tolerate in my life?

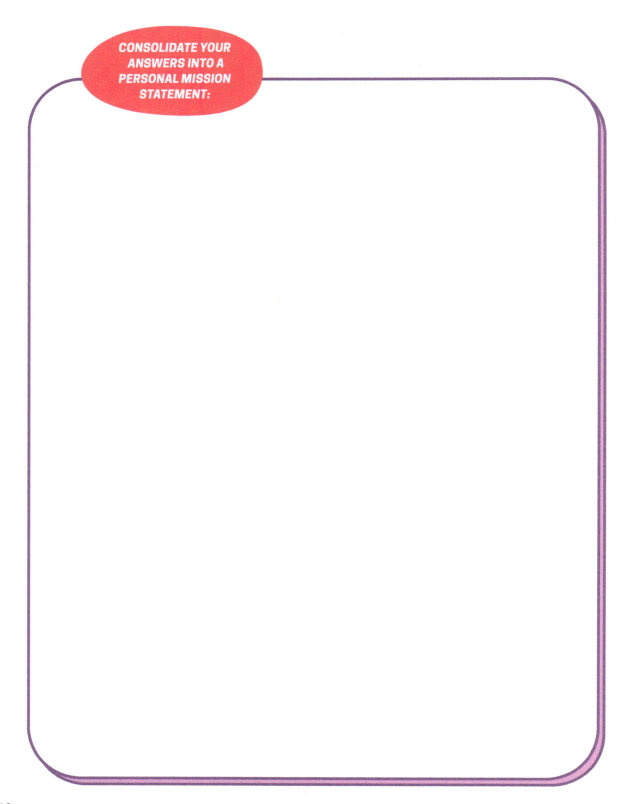

CONSOLIDATE YOUR ANSWERS INTO A PERSONAL MISSION STATEMENT:

DEVELOPING AN ELEVATOR PITCH

1. Read the introduction

2. Review sample personal elevator pitches provided here

3. Heed the tips provided for writing

4. Identify the resources available to you for support

5. Answer the questions provided to develop the pitch

6. Consolidate your answers into a personal elevator pitch

INTRODUCTION:

A personal elevator pitch is a short, clear, concise message about yourself, a commercial for you. It communicates who you are, what you do, and how you benefit a company or organization. It is usually under 30 seconds, the time it takes to ride an elevator. The pitch should be 80 words or less, 8 sentences maximum, and is structured to spark the interest of the audience, whether one or many. It is also a way to easily answer the question: "So tell me a little about yourself?" giving you the confidence to elaborate if asked. It provides you with a comfortable way to introduce yourself at any time, anywhere, once again providing you with the competence, courage, and calm to present yourself in any setting.

41

"I AM A CREATIVE PASSIONATE, **HIGH ENERGY** GRAPHIC DESIGNER AT XYZ COMPANY. MY TEAM HAS WON SEVERAL XYZ AWARDS AND I'M ALWAYS LOOKING FOR THE MOST EXCITING AND EFFECTIVE SOLUTIONS FOR OUR CLIENTS, SUCH AS XYZ COMPANY. I HAVE A MASTER'S DEGREE IN MANAGEMENT, WHICH ALLOWS ME TO EFFECTIVELY DIRECT A WIDE RANGE OF EMPLOYEES AND OUTSIDE VENDORS."

TIPS TO CONSIDER WHILE WRITING THE PITCH:

- Write down everything that comes to mind that helps identify who you are: Name, Occupation, Position, Possible future position title.
- Connect the phrases to each other so they flow naturally and smoothly.
- Time the pitch and edit as many times as necessary until you are comfortable.
- Memorize and practice, practice, practice, until you are comfortable. Try presenting the pitch in front of a friend or colleague, and in front of a mirror.
- Eliminate unnecessary information and words and focus on making short powerful sentences.
- Make sure the language sounds like you.
- Remember the listener wants to know "What's in it for me?"

PERSONAL ELEVATOR PITCH RESOURCES

What will help me write this pitch?

What could hinder me from completing the pitch?

What specific actions can I take to help me complete the pitch?

Are there people who can help me?

What dates can I commit to: start writing?

PERSONAL ELEVATOR PITCH WORKSHEET

Who am I? (I am Joan Smith and I...)

What business or service do I provide?

What is my specific field of expertise?

What is my current position?

In what capacity do I serve? (what exactly do I do?)

Is there a specific highlight to your career *(I have received commendations from xyz organization for my work as a (writer, speaker, teacher, executive, etc.)?*

What is my Unique Selling Proposition? *(What makes you different from the competition?)*

What benefits do my customer/clients derive from my service?

What benefits can my employer derive from my skills, based on proven accomplishments?

Is there a specific goal you aspire to? This is optional, but helpful if you have a specific career goal. *(I am an award-winning writer who aspires to be the head creative director at xyz magazine.)*

CONSOLIDATE YOUR ANSWERS INTO A PERSONAL ELEVATOR PITCH:

FAITH-BASED LEADERSHIP

HOW CAN YOUR FAITH HELP IN YOUR LEADERSHIP JOURNEY?

"I love Jesus but I Cuss a Little!" I saw this t-shirt while engaging in one of my favorite distractions, scrolling through Facebook. When I saw the t-shirt, I laughed out loud. In a humorous way, it describes the interesting tension many leaders, including me, face as they lead and use religious principles in the process.

My parents were committed to ensuring their daughters had the foundation of faith as they developed us into confident women leaders. They created opportunities for us to choose the religion that most resonated with us as we matured. The Webber girls visited churches of different denominations. We were allowed to ask questions of friends and families with religious and spiritual practices different from ours. This helped us each choose a religion that aligned most with what we came to believe as women leaders.

Be confident, competent, courageous, and calm in the pursuit of your purpose

My religious journey is quite interesting. I always believed in something greater than me. I believe that Jesus Christ is the thing greater than me. I reflect on Christian principles as I live and lead. In 2006 a brief conversation with my Pastor Robert E. Wilson, Roosevelt Memorial Baptist Church, led to the incorporation of Gwen, Inc. He inspired me to read Jeremiah 29:11 "For I know the plans I have for you," declares the Lord, "plans to prosper you and not to harm you, plans to give you hope and a future." This scripture gave me the courage to translate an idea I incubated for ten years into a thriving business. I stand on this scripture with every business decision I make. I prayed and believed myself into being the President/CEO of Gwen, Inc.

Being a Christian requires something simple of me - Love God and to love others in the unconditional way God loves them too. To be honest, doing this daily is one of my greatest challenges, and where that cussing thing comes into play (LOL!) Like many leaders there are days I lose my marbles at home and in my company on people who just work my last good nerve! Thank God for forgiveness. I hit the reset button and begin again.

During conversations with leaders, there is a point when faith is discussed as a strategic leadership resource. There are faith-based practices common to clients regardless of their chosen religion. It is important to know their leadership left the world a better place upon their death.

Prayer is a part of the day. Having a prayer practice allows the opportunity to meditate on important issues. Prayer is where they ask for guidance to lead their businesses.

These leaders believe forgiveness is critical to business success. They believe in "Do Overs." When mistakes are made they make corrections, forgive the errors and inspire employees to try again.

They act on the concept that faith and earthly works make the difference in their businesses. Leaders have faith that business goals will be achieved, yet know faith only comes to fruition when employees run day-to-day operations effectively.

These leaders are deeply concerned about their legacies while on earth. All of my clients want to hear their religion's version of "a job well done, my good and faithful servant" when they arrive in heaven.

My company's tag line "Because Leadership Is Not A Job to Do Alone" refers to the need to engage the support of others while leading on earth. For me and many other leaders "not doing it alone" also means leaning on faith while leading. Leaders hesitate to discuss faith as an important leadership resource. I don't believe religion should be imposed on others. However, I strongly encourage leaders to acknowledge the role of faith in giving them a little extra something to lead a successful business.

I pray daily for leaders. We have important work to do and a little help from above is not a bad thing.

SPACE FOR REFLECTION

FAMILY OVER EVERYTHING

WHEN WAS THE LAST TIME YOU THANKED
YOUR FAMILY FOR SUPPORTING THE
WORK YOU DO AS A LEADER?

Thanksgiving is my favorite holiday. I love to spend time with family and friends eating the annual Team Webber-McLeod Soul Food Extravaganza. But even more important to me is recognizing that Thanksgiving is a time I give extra thanks for those who assist me in being the President/CEO of Gwen, Inc. I am only able to live out my wildest entrepreneurial dreams because of the unconditional support I receive from family, friends and the Gwen, Inc. team. I especially thank my family because although my work gives our family many benefits, supporting me requires much of them.

RELATIONSHIPS REALLY MATTER

When was the last time you thanked your family for supporting the work you do as a leader? I encourage leaders to think about the role family plays in one's quest to be an outstanding leader. As corny as it may sound, every successful leader I support speaks of the family as the "wind beneath their wings."

As leaders, we must never forget families are our biggest cheerleaders, executive coaches, and the centers of calm in our lives. We cannot be all we are without their unconditional love, understanding, and tolerance of our constant counterbalancing of work and home activities. We must give thanks to our families for believing in us, especially when it is hard as leaders to believe in ourselves. In return, leaders must slow down enough to acknowledge all the family does in support of their careers. Leaders must demonstrate in word, action, and deed that

FAMILY OVER EVERYTHING.

In the busy-ness of leadership, it is easy to forget that careers affect our spouses, partners, significant others, and children. They are the recipients of joy when things go well. They are equally the recipients of stress when things don't go well. Leaders must be thoughtful about building relationships that allow our families to understand what is required of everyone to achieve career aspirations. Leaders must remain open to feedback regarding how career aspirations affect the family. The Webber-McLeods frequently tell me about the good they receive from my career choices.

However, they are equally permitted to tell me when it is difficult to be the husband or child of Gwen Webber-McLeod the woman, entrepreneur and community leader. I am sure this family dynamic resonates with other leaders too.

More and more, leaders express concern about the tension careers cause the family. Unchecked, this tension causes significant damage to family relationships. What can leaders do to reduce this tension?

Live life with mission and purpose!

I RECOMMEND BEING PROACTIVE

Involve your family as soon as you embark on the leadership journey. Explain career aspirations to them in great detail. Help the family understand your day-to-day work.

Share feelings with them when things are great and difficult.

Develop family strategies and messages for dealing with the backlash that might occur when something you do plays out in public. Hold family meetings to simply check in with each other.

Be willing not to do something if your family feels the impact causes more harm than good to them.

Ask your family for support.

Finally, use Thanksgiving to give extra thanks to your family for all they do in support of your leadership. But remember to give them thanks always; they should never be confused about how much you honor their contributions to your success.

In the end, there is no leadership relationship more important than the one you have with family. Leaders soar because loved ones are willing to be the "wind beneath their wings." The "lift" received from loved ones truly inspires us to new levels of leadership.

Remember during holidays and always, **family over everything.**

Inspirational Poem: Before you continue your learning, reflect for a moment on

READY TO UNFOLD
BY MONA LAKE JONES, FROM THE COLOR OF CULTURE II

Stand back and watch me
I'm getting ready to unfold!
I've decided to let my spirit go free
I'm ready to become the woman I was meant to be.
I've either been somebody's daughter, mother or wife
And now it's time for me to take charge of my life.
I've been pondering all this time trying to decide just who I am
At first, I thought it depended on whether I had a man.
Then I thought that simply just because
Others had more seniority; they could decide who I was.
I played all the roles that were expected and
I seldom asked why I've had my wings closed up,
but now I'm ready to fly
I've been awakened and I finally see the light
I'm about to make some changes
and set a few things right.
With my new attitude and the knowledge I possess
I might create a whole new world order
and clean up all this mess!
Stand back and watch me
I'm just getting ready to unfold!

55

RESULTS OF LEARNING: SECTION ONE

Now that you have read the essays, completed your worksheets, considered the resource essays, and reflected on the powerful words of Mona Lake Jones, think about how you will answer this question:

AS A RESULT OF MY LEARNING EXPERIENCE IN SECTION ONE, HOW WILL THIS KNOWLEDGE HELP ME BECOME THE LEADER I ASPIRE TO BE?

Take time to identify the answer to the question above, identifying at least one action you can take in your own leadership life as a direct result of completing Section One. Also write down any concerns, situations or questions which your reading has helped you identity. The space on the next page provides you with an opportunity to collect all your thoughts in one place, which will be helpful later in completing your Personal Leadership Plan.

SPACE FOR REFLECTION

INTRODUCTION TO SECTION TWO

CLEAR YOUR PATH: ACQUIRING FUNDAMENTAL LEADERSHIP SKILLS

Leaders must have specific technical skills to do well in their positions; but there are other human skills that must be developed to be an effective leader. These skills focus on building and leveraging relationships with employees and colleagues. Every success or failure you experience as a leader is connected to a relationship with someone else. Understanding the impact of relationships on trust, communicating effectively, and working with others during life's most significant challenges is critical to your success.

Clearing your path of obstacles lets you develop various skill sets which contribute to leadership success and gives leaders confidence. Clear your head, heart, and spirit of people and things that zap your energy. Get rid of dream-killers.

A woman can't live and lead with confidence, competence, courage, and calm surrounded by people who derail her life vision. Minimize your interactions with those who do not share your vision, and keep your life focused on positives.

Acquiring certain skills and understanding core issues will also give you the confidence you need to advance both your personal life and career. The essays, worksheets, and resource documents provide you with fundamental skills to help you move forward with more confidence toward your goals.

Employing these skills as part of your daily leadership will give you confidence. As you read each article, remember to use the space provided to make notes, ask questions of yourself, write down concerns.

ESSAYS:

TRUST
Trust is the glue that bonds a leader to a team and the team together.

COMMUNICATION STYLES
Understanding how you communicate and recognizing the communication style of others can be a powerful tool in your success.

UNDERSTANDING FEEDBACK
Having skill in both giving and receiving feedback will increase your leadership effectiveness.

WORKSHEETS

DETERMINING YOUR COMMUNICATION STYLE
Understanding how we communicate with others can help our leadership success. This worksheet lets you determine your primary communication style and recognize the styles of others.

HAVING DIFFICULT CONVERSATIONS
Following these steps in planning a difficult conversation will give you confidence in communication. These tools can improve your communication effectiveness in both personal and business relationships.

 Defining the Necessary Conversation Worksheet

 Having the Conversation You Don't Want to Have Worksheet

RESOURCE ARTICLES:

IT'S PERSONAL
Leaders are concerned about the challenge of being good ethical people while tending to the tasks of leading successful businesses.

NOTHING TO DO BUT DECIDE
Leaders are required to make decisions all through their careers, but because these decisions affect others in the organization, decision making can be a huge challenge for the leader.

LEADING THROUGH GRIEF
Living through grief is one of the more challenging human conditions. This experience is amplified when one is responsible for leading others.

INSPIRATIONAL POEM:
Quote by Eleanor Roosevelt

RESULTS OF LEARNING:
Use the inspirational poem to help you focus on how your behavior will change as a result of working in this section. Write down specific actions you will take, any concerns or situations hindering your path to success.

TRUST:

T=C+I (TRUST= CREDIBILITY + INTIMACY)

WHAT IS TRUST?
WHAT MUST A LEADER DO TO BE VIEWED AS TRUSTWORTHY BY HER/HIS EMPLOYEES?
WHAT FACTORS CONTRIBUTE TO A HIGH LEVEL OF TRUST ON A TEAM?

To help leaders think about the topic of trust I use an equation to set a working definition:

T=C+I, TRUST EQUALS CREDIBILITY PLUS INTIMACY

This equation provides an easy framework for leaders interested in being trustworthy and building trust in a team. When you break the equation down it identifies what is required of an individual leader who wants to be known as trustworthy.

CREDIBILITY

speaks to the importance of leaders doing what they say they will do. I often tell leaders their employees study them like science projects. They know your every move. They decide whether or not to trust you based on these observations over time. Leaders must be consistent in word, action, and deed. I refer to this as understanding the perception of your patterns of word and deed alignment. In short, does your body consistently follow what your mouth is saying? When it does, these repeated behaviors say something about who you are and support people's ability to trust you. This opens the door for the next component of the trust equation intimacy.

INTIMACY

speaks to the importance of leaders allowing themselves to be known and understood by people in the workplace. This does not mean leaders have to share all their personal business. It does however, encourage leaders to let people know who they are and to make clear their principles.

Building intimacy requires a leader to be open to questions, comments, concerns and respectful criticism. Intimacy develops when leaders share goals, values, and beliefs with colleagues and employees. Intimacy leads to relationship building and relationships really matter when building trust.

Create a circle of sisterhood

Understanding the connection between credibility and intimacy is important to the individual leader desiring to be known as trustworthy. It is also the leader's task to set the tone for trust in a team. Given this, it is helpful to be aware of behaviors that contribute to building and maintaining trust in a team:

- ESTABLISHING AND MAINTAINING INTEGRITY BETWEEN AND AMONG TEAM MEMBERS

- COMMUNICATING VISION AND VALUES FOR THE TEAM

- CONSIDERING ALL EMPLOYEES AS EQUAL PARTNERS

- FOCUSING ON SHARED NOT PERSONAL GOALS FOR TEAM MEMBERS

- DOING WHAT'S RIGHT FOR THE TEAM EVEN WHEN THERE MAY BE PERSONAL RISK

Research on leadership has found the absence of trust leads to team dysfunction. Behavior that destroys trust in a team:

High performing teams have a high level of trust between the leader and the team, and among team members. On these teams' trust is a business resource that is treated the same as other important business resources.

If you are interested in improving as a leader and/or developing a high-performance team don't forget to include the topic of trust in this process.

Trust is the glue that bonds a leader to a team and the team together.

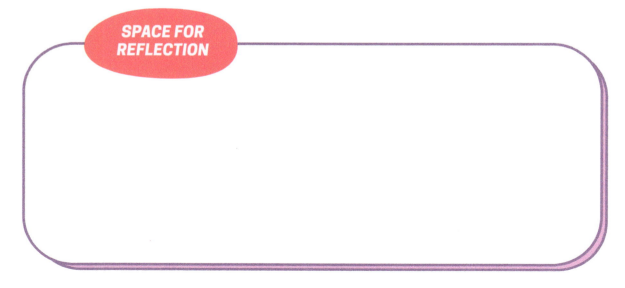

UNDERSTANDING COMMUNICATION STYLES

HOW DOES UNDERSTANDING THE WAY WE COMMUNICATE HELP OUR LEADERSHIP?

Have you ever sat in a meeting and wondered "why is she acting this way?" Sometimes I'm thinking: is it just a bad day for someone, or is this behavior an example of how they lead? What if you could easily understand the way people communicate, how you interact with them, respect the differences in others, and get everyone to act in harmony?

When you are in a work-meeting, or having a social engagement, or even just a conversation with a friend or family member, you have probably noticed that some people want to tell you what they know, others are more interested in asking questions, some are more active in a meeting, some are quiet and thoughtful.

In my work with leaders, I help them recognize how important it is to genuinely listen to encourage open and honest communications, to give and take respectful criticism, and to understand that most people fall into general communication categories.

When you as a leader begin to understand this, you can improve your effectiveness and that of your team. This understanding also applies to your personal life and can help you understand the actions and behaviors of family and friends.

Understanding different styles of communicating, and recognizing the behaviors associated with each, can contribute to your personal leadership development, helping you with insights to others. This knowledge will help you understand behavior in a non-judgmental way, accepting and adjusting your own responses.

The next time you are in one of "those" conversations or meetings, try to recognize the communication styles of your colleagues and adjust your input accordingly. You will have more successful meetings, relationships, and outcomes if you keep in mind these three maxims:

FEEDBACK

HAVE YOU EVER THOUGHT ABOUT FEEDBACK AS "THE GIFT THAT KEEPS ON GIVING?"

I love the holiday season. There is something truly beautiful about observing traditions across faiths and communities during this special time of year. What I enjoy most about the season is the spirit of giving that is common to every tradition. Considering this in the context of leadership makes me think about a gift employees can give to leaders. This gift is frequent and consistent feedback. Open, honest feedback is a gift that keeps on giving.

It is my experience that most employees desire to provide feedback to leaders. However, they frequently withhold feedback out of fear they will be punished if leaders don't like what is said. Unfortunately, this is a reality that employees live with all too often. Many leaders have low tolerance for open and honest feedback and "kill" messengers who muster the courage to offer feedback for consideration.

LIFE IS TOO SHORT TO PLAY WITH YOUR DREAMS

Leaders must reflect on their capacity for feedback. Feedback is the "breakfast of champions" in my book. Developing the capacity to actively seek and receive feedback is central to the success of every leader. It is equally important to help employees understand the many ways feedback can be given and make it safe for feedback to be given.

I find certain strategies for obtaining feedback are more effective than others. These strategies create safe ways for employees to provide great feedback to leaders.

COMPANY SURVEYS

Surveys that are developed with care are great tools for identifying internal issues, perceptions about leaders, and levels of employee engagement. Employees are more apt to be open when assured the survey process is anonymous. It is important to identify major survey themes and share them with employees. Provide specific information about how the feedback will be used. The goal is to use the process to set the tone that employee feedback is valued by the company. The critical piece of the process is to have word-deed alignment regarding how feedback will be used. Employees will continue to give feedback when they "see" their input used in the company.

CHALLENGING UP AND SUPPORTING OUT

is another strategy that makes it safe for mid-managers to provide feedback to leaders. This strategy requires leaders to permit managers to openly challenge ideas, pending decisions and policies in meetings. The challenges must be fact-based, topic-specific, focused on outcomes and respectful. This strategy allows for issues to be worked out in advance so a "united front" among leaders and managers is shown when decisions or policies are shared with employees. This strategy is effective when consensus is needed among direct reports for a decision or policy to be effective. A benefit of this strategy is it allows leaders to demonstrate the capacity for receiving feedback face-to-face. Managers need to see this capacity to believe it.

INTERNAL FOCUS GROUPS

allow leaders to meet with employees in small groups to develop a deeper understanding of perspectives about company issues. Employees are randomly selected or strategically organized based on the type of feedback being solicited. Focus groups work best when designed and managed by leaders with strong facilitation skills.

Focus group questions must be very clear and specific to ensure desired levels of employee response. Following the focus group process, it is important to share major themes and how employee feedback will be used in the company. The beauty of focus groups is they enable employees to be "up close and personal" with leaders while hearing how other employees feel about company issues, too.

LEADING BY "WALKING AROUND"

is another way to obtain feedback. Sometimes leaders need to just walk around the company informally soliciting employee feedback. This "walking around" must be planned, intentional and authentic. Leaders engaged in this strategy announce that they will be visiting certain areas to have brief interactions with employees. These interactions focus on informal conversations, seeking new ideas, and looking for ideas to improve the work of a department. Employees enjoy it when leaders visit their departments. It demonstrates that leaders care about the day-to-day work of the company. It also reduces a common employee complaint, "We never see managers and leaders in our departments." Seeing managers and leaders in the workplace sends a signal to employees that the company cares about them and appreciates the specific work they do.

Employees have so much to offer a company in terms of skill, knowledge, and wisdom. These valuable resources are often wasted because leaders fail to seek input and feedback. Carry the spirit of this season into the new year. Create the opportunity for employees to give the gift that keeps on giving year-round - open, honest feedback.

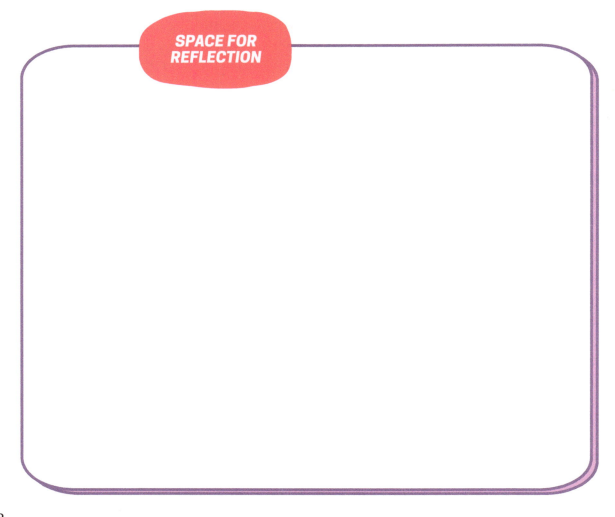

SPACE FOR REFLECTION

DETERMINING YOUR COMMUNICATION STYLE WORKSHEET:

INTRODUCTION:
Knowing the four basic communication styles, learning to recognize your style, and those of your work team and family can help you have confidence in communication for the best success. The language in our worksheet is from the ***Social Styles Model of Communication,*** originated by David Merrill and Roger Reid in their book: ***Personal Styles and Effective Performance*** and is based upon the psychology of Carl Jung.

Research shows there are four basic styles of communication:

THE DRIVER
will trust facts, data, and coherent arguments. They want proof before making decisions and are mostly 'bottom line' doers who mistrust vague or emotive ideas. They enjoy power and while they are not necessarily domineering, they like to seize hold of a situation to influence others to see things their way.

THE ANALYTICAL
is also rational and proof orientated. They are often quieter, more thoughtful types who are less inclined to act with the same assurance or self-confidence as the driver and will prefer to advise, consult or theorize. They do not welcome risk or challenge to the same extent and tend to work better under instructions. Compatible with the driver.

THE EXPRESSIVE
is an emotional person who will often act on a strong idea or inspiration, fueled by the belief that it feels right. At worst they are impulsive and unpredictable, at best they are creative and highly inspirational. They are people-orientated and enjoy interaction but also enjoy being the center of attention and the one in the 'limelight.'

THE AMIABLE is also an emotional individual, driven largely by what they feel. They are highly sensitive to others and are interested in well-being and prize relationships highly. Acceptance is a key for them. While they are not overly insecure, they enjoy comfort and safety and dislike too much pressure. Not motivated by the desire to lead, but like the Analytical, are happy under guidance. Extremely good listeners, they can sometimes show 'submissive' tendencies.

The labels are not as important as the behavior. The words are meant to not reflect values or biases. It is important to remember that great leaders, managers, and employees are represented by each of these styles.

The following worksheet will help you determine your basic style. Remember that you are capable of acting in all these styles, but one will emerge as dominant.

MERRILL–REID SOCIAL COMMUNICATION MODEL: DESCRIBING MY TYPICAL BEHAVIOR

Directions:

For each pair of statements below, select one statement that most closely "fits" YOUR OBSERVABLE BEHAVIOR when you are communicating or making decisions with others.

Circle the letter to the left of the statement that best "fits."

A
Use relatively few, but controlled gestures and body movements

OR

B
Use many, sweeping gestures, head nodding, and body movements

L
Lean back, think about what others are saying, making occasional eye contact

OR

R
Lean forward, face the other squarely, and hold eye contact

R
Use quick, fast-paced speech, strong speech

OR

L
Use slow-paced, deliberate (sometimes cautious) speech

B
Have very responsive, animated facial expression (frowns, smiles, etc.)

OR

A
Remain generally unresponsive in facial expression, or not changing expression

R
Speak more loudly

OR

L
Speak more softly

A

Be cautious, careful, and use factual information (with back-up data) in meetings and presentations

OR

B

Be open and active, express opinions fully, often without giving specific detail

L

Make sure of facts or the effect on others before taking a firm stand on an issue

OR

R

Emphasize points, make decision, take stand (let the chips fall where they may)

B

Be playful, joking, bantering

OR

A

Be serious, thoughtful, and logical

L

Not make the final decision until considering the alternatives and the politics (personalities) in the situation

OR

R

Decide and act on information and feeling right now

A

Be more task-oriented

OR

B

Be more people-oriented

RECORD THE NUMBER OF TIMES YOU CIRCLED THE LETTERS:

A ☐ **B** ☐

RECORD THE NUMBER OF TIMES YOU CIRCLED THE LETTERS:

L ☐ **R** ☐

COMBINE THE TWO LETTERS WITH HIGHEST NUMBERS
(EXAMPLE: AR)

IDENTIFY YOUR STYLE BELOW

AL=ANALYTIC
AR=DRIVER
BL=AMIABLE
BR=EXPRESSIVE

MY PRIMARY COMMUNICATING STYLE APPEARS TO BE:

☐

THIS QUESTIONNAIRE SEEMS TO AGREE WITH MY PERCEPTION OF MYSELF:

☐	☐	☐	☐
RIGHT ON	**REASONABLY WELL**	**OK**	**NOT AT ALL**

HAVING DIFFICULT CONVERSATIONS

INTRODUCTION:
They're not always easy, but the hardest conversations can strengthen your most cherished relationships, both in your career and personal life. Mastering tools to help you communicate in difficult situations can substantially reduce your anxiety in addressing difficult conversations. The communication tools/practice sheets below give you simple and direct directions for engaging in these hard conversations.

- Defining the Necessary Conversation Worksheet
- Having the Conversation You Don't Want to Have Worksheet

THE NECESSARY CONVERSATION
by Leslie Rose McDonald, Pathfinders CTS Inc., 2004. In your leadership career, there will be times when you need to have a necessary conversation with an employee, colleague, friend or family member. It is important to carefully plan; using these steps below will provide you the perspective for the necessary conversation.

Directions:
Using the questions on the next pages, draft your plan to have a necessary conversation. Think about a specific issue you want to address when answering.

With whom do you need to have a necessary conversation?

How long is this conversation overdue?

What has been the benefit to you for not addressing it?

What has been the impact on your energy of not addressing this issue?

Why do you think you have chosen to avoid this conversation?

Are you ready now? Why or why not?

What assistance/resources will you need to feel prepared to have your necessary conversation?

How will you feel once you have had this conversation?

How will you hold yourself accountable to follow through with this commitment?

HAVING THE CONVERSATION YOU DON'T WANT TO HAVE

How often have you been concerned about a problem, situation or relationship, but keep putting off doing something about it? In both our personal and professional lives, it sometimes becomes necessary to "have the conversation you don't want to have." You know you need to clear the air, suggest solutions, and go forward with a better communication path, but are reluctant to begin. You can have success with this type of conversation if you carefully prepare, control your fear of failure, and approach it with an open mind. Below is a worksheet which will help you plan for this conversation.

Directions:
Following is a recommended framework for preparing for difficult conversations. Identify a situation in your life you need to address and use these steps to make your plan for the difficult conversation.

1. Identify the problem as specifically as possible, and the person in question.

Problem:

Person:

2. Set a blueprint or process for the shared talk. Spend some time developing an agenda for how you want the conversation to go. Keep it short and to the point. Write out your plan or process:

3. Contact the person for a mutual time to discuss the issue. State your concern as simply and diplomatically as possible in this request.

Practice writing your request:

4. Ask the person to accept the request, and make comments or respectful criticisms to your agenda. Remember you are looking to have a shared conversation, not a one-way dialog you direct.

5. Once you agree on the process, begin the conversation, looking for clues to their behavior, and listening with patience and an open mind. State your own concerns without judging the other person. Your first comments and tone will set the stage for conversation.

SOME TIPS FOR YOUR CONVERSATION

DON'T FORGET THEY WILL BE AS NERVOUS AS YOU ARE.

TAKE NOTES ON THE SOLUTION YOU CREATE TOGETHER.

SEND THE SOLUTION, AND ASK FOR AGREEMENT. MAKE MODIFICATIONS IF NECESSARY.

SEND YOUR SINCERE THANKS AND PRAISE TO YOU BOTH FOR BEING WILLING TO TAKE ON THE ISSUE.

6. Practice your opening lines to begin the conversation below: What will you say first?:

IT'S PERSONAL

DO YOU RECOGNIZE THE CONNECTION
BETWEEN WHO YOU ARE, WHAT YOU DO,
AND YOUR ABILITY TO INSPIRE OTHERS?

"Leadership development requires a willingness to engage in personal and spiritual work." This statement was made during a gathering at my home in 2007 during which I revealed intentions to create a leadership development corporation. My initial reaction was, "Oh my, how will I ever get leaders to accept the work they need to do to be effective in business?" Years later I've discovered that leaders are perfectly willing to accept this notion and truly want to do this work.

I serve as a professional mentor and process partner to many leaders throughout the state. Typically, I am engaged to help them become stronger leaders and to process business issues. During sessions, focus is primarily on the "hard" side of business. However, at some point the conversation always becomes personal. Leaders are deeply concerned about being good ethical people while tending to the tasks of leading successful businesses and organizations. They recognize the connection between who they are, what they believe, what they do and the ability to inspire employees to achieve business goals.

When the conversation becomes personal leaders talk about their lives, families, friends, and work. They have breakthroughs about past relationships and the effect they have on their leadership today. They open up about challenges, failures and regrets. They discuss the role religion or spiritual practices play in leadership. They consult me regarding strategies for righting past wrongs. They truly desire to be authentically human as they lead each day.

I am constantly intrigued by the clarity and courage that emerges when people realize it is possible to be authentically human and an excellent leader at the same time. Many think leadership means showing no emotion, never apologizing, being right all the time, setting rules for employees that don't apply to them and living in a "my way or the highway" philosophy. People believe this is what excellent leadership looks like because unfortunately it is a model frequently celebrated in communities, states, and countries. I refer to this as the "veneer of leadership." It is what many put on and polish because they believe this is what leaders do. Yet in the many years I've specialized in providing direct support to individual leaders I've never worked with a "veneered" leader who is successful and feels good about their work. I find these individuals stressed, exhausted and dealing with low trust/low performing organizations because they are personally a mess and can't inspire people to follow them.

It may seem counter-intuitive for leaders to engage in personal and spiritual work at a time when businesses struggle with complex issues. I offer this is the ideal time to look inward. Everything that happens in business occurs through the relationships leaders have with themselves and then with employees. Employees get cues for how to respond during difficult times from watching what leaders do.

Everything a leader is, believes, says, and does affects the success of a business. Given this, it is imperative for leaders to know their head, heart, and spirit and to share this information as appropriate with employees. When employees know a leader, they trust them and will follow them most anywhere.

YOU GET WHAT YOU ARE IN LEADERSHIP

If leaders desire positive business outcomes from employees, they must be positive, smart, inspiring, and authentically human people. Take time for personal and spiritual work. Pause for self-reflection. The better a leader takes care of their head, heart, and spirit, the better the business will be.

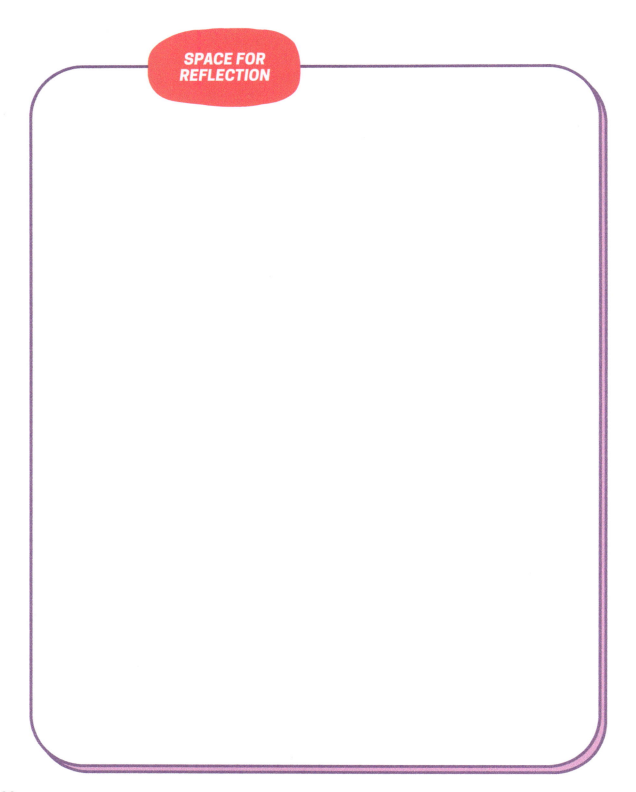

SPACE FOR REFLECTION

NOTHING LEFT TO DO BUT DECIDE

WHY IS DECISION MAKING SO DIFFICULT?

The capacity to make decisions is fundamental to being an effective leader. However, one of the most difficult moments in leadership is the point when there is nothing left to do but decide. I see leaders get right to the "edge" of decision-making and freeze up. Many second guess themselves. Others change a decision they know is right. Some throw out the decision completely. Why is decision making so difficult?

Decisions always affect other people. This contributes to the difficulty. Successfully executing a decision requires leaders to create a culture of cooperation among those who will be affected by decisions. Decisions always lead to change. Change makes people fearful and uneasy. These difficulties are captured in one of my favorite quotes from Niccolò Machiavelli, in his 16th century political treatise, *The Prince*. "There is nothing more difficult to take in hand, more perilous to conduct, or more uncertain in its success, than to take the lead in the introduction of a new order of things." Dealing with the fall out of this dynamic is enough to make any leader stop short of deciding.

QUESTIONS TO CONSIDER

It is my experience that leaders who are fearless about decision-making are those who understand the "art" of effective decision making and execution. These leaders know the importance of advance planning for engaging others in decision-making. They consider how decisions should be made to obtain cooperation from those affected by the decision. For example:

Processing these questions in advance helps leaders identify strategies for engaging others in the decision-making process.

PROCESS IS IMPORTANT

The decision-making process is of equal importance. Typically, teams identify problems then hastily converge to find answers and move to action. On the surface, this process looks efficient. However, experts on decision-making find this process full of gaps. A more effective way to approach decision making begins with framing the problem so it is understood by those making the decision.

It helps to ask the decision-makers to look at the problem then identify "what success would look like" if the problem were solved. Once this is established those involved in the process can gather information to be considered in resolving the problem and to draw conclusions for the decisions that must be made to address the problem.

The final phase of this process includes learning from the decision-making experience so future processes can be improved.

ASSESSING TRAPS

Certain traps emerge during decision-making that leaders must know about and address. Knowing these traps and addressing them in the decision-making process enhances the quality of decisions.

GROUPTHINK is quite common. This results when faulty decisions are made as the result of group pressure.

OVERCONFIDENCE occurs when we think we know more than we do.

HEURISTIC THINKING occurs when we believe that what worked in the past will work again.

IRRATIONAL ESCALATION to commitment involves groups or individuals increasing commitment to bad decisions due to a desire to protect reputations.

These traps have damaging effects on decisions. They must be addressed quickly so the best decisions can be made.

THE FINAL DECISION

Leaders make hundreds of decisions daily. It is easy to understand the trepidation they experience as they consider the effect of their decisions on others. But there is no avoiding it, leaders must make decisions. When there is nothing left to do but decide, it is far easier to move forward when a leader understands the components required to make effective decisions that can be successfully executed.

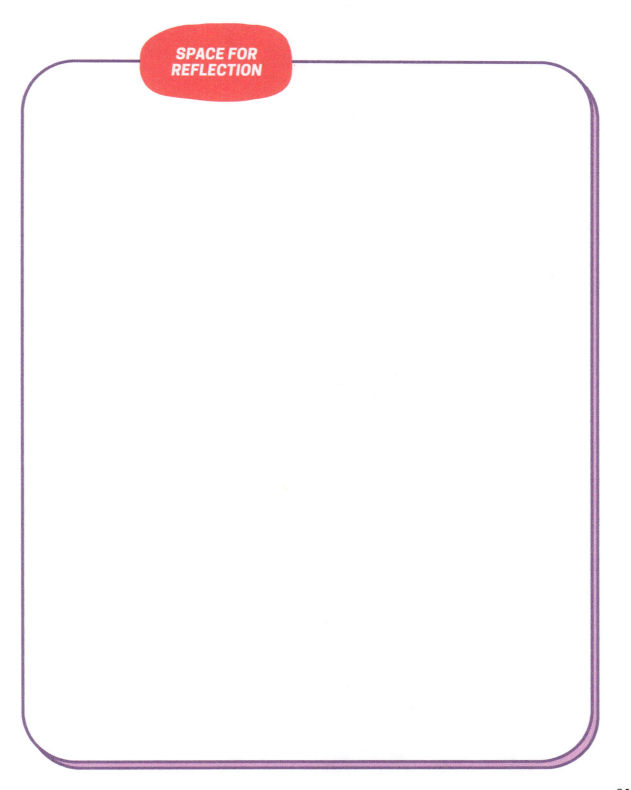

SPACE FOR REFLECTION

LEADING THROUGH GRIEF AND SORROW

HOW CAN LEADERS LEAD SUCCESSFULLY THROUGH A SEASON OF GRIEF?

Grief is a powerful emotion. It never really goes away. There is no such thing as full closure. Grief simply gets easier to manage as our hearts heal from losing someone we love. I am a bit of an expert on the topic of leading through grief and sorrow, as there was a ten-year period in my life that I describe as my season of grief. During this time, I supported family members experiencing life-changing events—divorces, health issues, job loss. During this period many of my close friends and family members died. There I was, a grief-stricken leader, trying to manage my professional responsibilities in this darkness. I often had grief on my mind as I reflected on current events that have many leaders throughout our country entering into their seasons of grief.

My company provides support to leaders who find themselves in the throes of grief and sorrow. We help them muster the courage to recognize that leading while managing grief is difficult but doable. We encourage these leaders to identify what they must do for themselves to sustain effectiveness when their hearts are breaking. Then we simply surround them with the support they need to step into each day delivering the expected business results. This may seem strange, but my personal experiences and working with grieving leaders enabled my team to identify what I describe as a set of practices that help those leading in times of grief and sorrow.

IT HELPS TO BE EDUCATED ABOUT
THE DYNAMICS AND POWER OF GRIEF.

Many fear that the physical, mental, and spiritual pain of grief will overcome them at any given moment. Here is the truth- there are times when it feels as if this pain will do just that. However, I observe when a leader understands that what they feel is normal they tend to be more willing to work with grief instead of fighting against it.

GRIEVING LEADERS MUST MAKE TIME TO GRIEVE.

Grieving leaders must make time to grieve. For example, I made appointments with my grief. I identified specific breaks in my schedule to do nothing else but rest and cry. Many leaders attempt to put grief aside while at work. Newsflash! Grief does not get out of the way just because someone is a leader; it becomes part of who the leader is and goes to work with them. I invite leaders to become students of their grief. Once the grief is understood, time at work can be orchestrated to support the need to grieve.

Grief is exhausting. Make sure to allocate time for rest and crying as needed during this powerful process. Emotions are part of the grieving process and must be released for healing to occur. Healing the hurt is what fuels the return to effective leadership.

BUSINESSES NEED TO FIND CREATIVE WAYS TO SUPPORT GRIEVING LEADERS.

Grief has a way of making leaders feel incompetent. Create access to internal and external support so the leader's quality of work can be sustained. It is important to demonstrate confidence in grieving leaders. It helps to know the business believes in them even when they are down. Leaders benefit from hearing specific examples of how they continue to do good work amid grieving. We encourage leaders to engage trusted advisors in the development of strategies to be used at work when grief takes over. Grief and sorrow can't be avoided in the workplace. It is best to know this and do what can be done to create environments that ease a leader's pain while they continue to do their work. To the grieving leader, remember that your darkness will turn into light in all due time. In the meantime, give yourself permission to settle into the grieving process and allow yourself to be supported as you learn to live without someone you love. I extend my deepest condolences to all grieving leaders. May the spirits of your loved ones' soar!

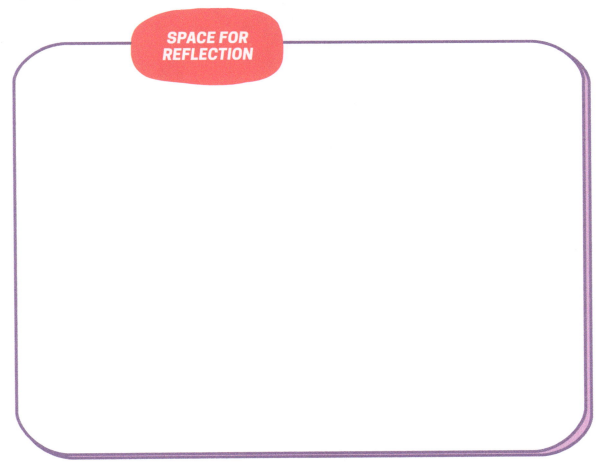

SPACE FOR REFLECTION

Inspirational Quote: Before you continue your learning, reflect for a moment on

You gain strength, courage, and confidence by every experience in which you really stop to look fear in the face.

~Eleanor Roosevelt

RESULTS OF LEARNING: SECTION TWO

Now that you have read the essays, completed your worksheets, considered the resource essays, and reflected on the inspiring words of Eleanor Roosevelt, think about how you will answer this question:

AS A RESULT OF YOUR LEARNING EXPERIENCE IN SECTION TWO, HOW WILL THIS KNOWLEDGE HELP ME BECOME THE LEADER I ASPIRE TO BE?

Take time to identify the answer to the question above, identifying at least one action you can take in your own leadership life as a direct result of completing Section Two. Also write down any concerns, situations or questions which your reading has helped you identify. The writing space below provides you with an opportunity to collect all your thoughts in one place, which will be helpful later in completing your Personal Leadership Plan.

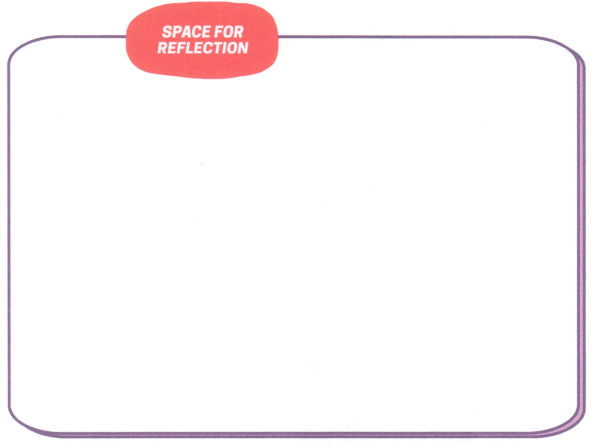

SPACE FOR REFLECTION

INTRODUCTION TO SECTION THREE

LEGACY BUILDING "INSPIRING A NEW GENERATION OF LEADERS"

All great leaders reflect on their careers, how they inspire and relate to others. Building a legacy of leadership begins the day you decide to lead. Everything you do leaves impressions on those following you. Live your leadership vision and communicate this as a mentor of future leaders. As you lead, take this realization into consideration. The awareness to build and sustain a legacy of leadership must be part of the leadership journey. Mentoring new generations, who will follow the values and philosophies you have lived as a leader, ensures successful continuity. You have discovered your personal leadership philosophy and learned fundamental skills, now you begin to acquire the knowledge to build a legacy of leadership that extends to new generations of leaders.

Who you are, how you live and lead, affect the future for you and those who come after.

ESSAYS:

LEGACY BUILDING
Our job as leaders is to be intentional about developing a legacy of leadership.

THE UNEXPECTED LEADER
Some leaders burst on the scene shaking things up and no one sees them coming.

UNBOUGHT, UNBOSSED, UNDAUNTED LEADERSHIP
It takes great courage to only engage in business activity that aligns with your beliefs, principles, and values.

CREDIBILITY
There is a direct connection between being credible and the ability to drive business results; it plays a significant role in building relationships that inspire others to follow your lead.

INFLUENCING OTHERS THROUGH MENTORING
One of the greatest leadership successes is the ability to positively influence the life of another.

WORKSHEET:

LEGACY BUILDING
Legacy Building: Visioning Exercise-This exercise provides an opportunity to think into the future, defining the characteristics of your leadership legacy.

RESOURCE ARTICLES:

EVERYDAY LEADERSHIP
"Everyday leaders" truly make a difference in our businesses, community, and the world.

WORK HARD, PLAY HARDER
Learning to be intentional about self-care helps your career success.

STAY ON TRACK
Dissatisfaction and fear about your position or leadership may make it difficult to stay on track in your career.

INSPIRATIONAL POEM:
"May The Work I've Done Speak for Me," by Sullivan Pugh, *The Consolers*

RESULTS OF LEARNING:
Use the inspirational quote to focus on how your behavior will change as a result of working in this section. Write down specific actions you will take, any concerns or situations hindering your path to success.

COMPILATION WORKSHEET:
Review the notes you have made from Sections 1-3 and compile them into one document for use in Section 4. You may notice trends or recurring themes and concerns. Organize them into groups or categories so you can find commonality.

BUILD A LEGACY OF LEADERSHIP

WHAT DOES IT MATTER IF YOU REACH LEADERSHIP CELEBRITY IF AT THE END OF YOUR CAREER YOU TURN AROUND AND CAN'T SEE THE MARK YOU LEFT IN LIFE?

Our job as leaders is to be intentional about developing a legacy of leadership. We should lead in ways that inspire new generations of leaders in our homes, companies, and communities. Successful leaders see themselves in service to others. Throughout their careers, they are intentional about leveraging their titles and experience to help others achieve success as leaders.

Successful leaders aren't haphazard about their legacies. They set an intention to use their careers to help others. The timing of legacy building is important. Every leader should consider this idea, however, only those who have long-term career experience have enough influence to open doors for others. As you strive to reach this professional place in your career, begin doing things to prepare you for this moment.

BUILD A SOLID PROFESSIONAL REPUTATION

Legacy building leaders spend years developing a personal brand that is respected by others. They have credibility at home, work, and in the community. They are known for having loyal followers. They are people who will do whatever is required in support of their leadership goals.

DEVELOP A FULL SET OF SKILLS

Legacy building leaders develop full competency in the technical skills needed in their chosen career. Using these skills, they develop the relationship-building skills that yield high trust/high performing strong bonds with others. They understand their success is directly tied to the quality of the connections they have with people in all aspects of life.

BEHAVE YOUR WAY TO SUCCESS

Throughout your career, people will hear what you say but only believe what they see you do. As a leader, your legacy is fundamentally grounded in whether your words and actions match. If you desire to inspire others to lead, it is imperative for you to show them what leadership looks like, not tell them. Walk your talk. Inspire trust. Extend trust to others. Be humble. Be a Servant Leader.

SEEK EVIDENCE ABOUT THE IMPACT OF YOUR LEADERSHIP

Legacy building leaders believe feedback is the breakfast of champions. In fact, they actively seek it from family, friends, and colleagues. They want to know if they are experienced as a leader in the way they desire to be experienced. Seek information that ensures there is congruence between your values, words, behaviors, and outcomes.

REFLECT AND REGROUP

Self-reflection is a critical aspect of building a legacy of leadership. Leadership is an ever-evolving process. In the process of building a legacy, it is important to acknowledge all aspects of the journey. Keep a journal to document important leadership lessons good or challenging. Reflect on these lessons. Use them to regroup as you build your legacy. Keep a listing of them to pass on to new generations of leaders.

PAY IT FORWARD

Paying your legacy forward is a term that is potentially cliché. Many say this is what they desire to do. However, few develop a specific plan for doing so. This action requires strategic intent. Paying your legacy of leadership forward requires one to do so "in and on purpose." Developing new generations of leaders requires a plan, a plan that identifies the details of how you intend to do this and for whom. What is the legacy you want to pass on? Who are the leaders you want to affect? What specific actions must you take to do so? Answering these questions ensures that your desire to pay it forward really happens in an impactful way. Let the legacy building begin! Develop a plan now that enables you to be an intentional leader who prepares new generations to lead with confidence, competence, courage, and calm.

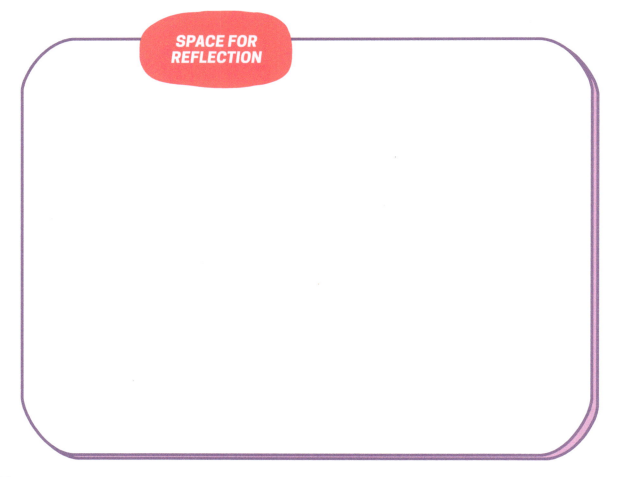

SPACE FOR REFLECTION

THE UNEXPECTED LEADER

ARE YOU AN UNEXPECTED LEADER?

Michele Obama, Kamala Harris, Harriet Tubman, Oprah—What do these women have in common? They are national examples of the "Unexpected Leader."

These leaders burst on the scene shaking things up and no one sees them coming. Their emergence as leaders is frequently met with shock, disbelief, and a lot of "it is not supposed to be your turn" energy and commentary!

I am intrigued by the unique leadership journey of women leaders of color. Throughout my career I've observed women leaders of color are not having the same professional experiences as their white male and female counterparts: this is especially true as it relates to access to leadership positions in companies and organizations. You will find that many companies are not always accustomed to viewing your demographic as leadership material.

My own leadership journey made me realize how often I am experienced as "unexpected," and how frequently my talents, skills and leadership are questioned because of my gender and race. This inspired me to think specifically about factors impacting professional women leaders of color, and I trademarked the phrase the "Unexpected Leader" to define this unique professional experience.

The Unexpected Leader is a professional woman of color who, upon hire or promotion, breaks the "cement" ceiling in a company or organization. Seldom is it "expected" for these women to achieve executive leader status However, when they do, this Unexpected Leader always exceeds expectations. The professional factor of "unexpectedness" sets off career-long dynamics professional women leaders of color must navigate:

- Being the First, Only and Different

- Struggling to gain and sustain credibility due to unchecked racism, sexism and microaggression in a company or organization culture.

- Deep desire to build a legacy that opens doors for women leaders of color following in their footsteps.

My personal goal is to ensure women leaders, especially women leaders of color, understand the dynamics of being an Unexpected Leader and how to overcome these factors to ensure career success. When you lead with confidence, competence, courage, and calm, you will certainly achieve your goals, and exceed all expectations. Keep these ideas in mind as you read the following article.

HONOR YOUR LEGACY.

ARE YOU THE UNEXPECTED LEADER?
If you are, I have a few tips for you.

BEING THE "FIRST & ONLY"

Prepare to pass the "first and only test." Being the "first and only" is an honor. But it comes with challenges you must prepare to face. I liken this experience to being the new exotic animal at the zoo. Everyone wants to see you because they've never seen a leader like you before. If you are the Unexpected Leader people will be curious about you. The Unexpected Leader must strategically introduce her/himself to the organization. It is important to honor the history of those who led before you. Connect to this leadership by sharing what you have in common with former leaders. Let people get to know you by sharing your communication style, beliefs, and values. Invite questions and respond to them openly and respectfully. Listen to and tap down fears about you.

Normalize your leadership early in your new position and then be consistent. Word deed alignment really matters when you are the Unexpected Leader.

SUSTAINING CREDIBILITY

Unexpected Leaders struggle to gain and sustain credibility. This struggle is seldom about qualifications. Each Unexpected Leader arrives in the position with the confidence, competence, courage, and calm to lead. However, when you are the Unexpected Leader people question your legitimacy, because in their minds it was not supposed to be you. Your ideas and decisions will be challenged. Your intellect and ability to lead will be suspect to some. You may even be blatantly disrespected. Try not to take any of this personally. The challenge to the Unexpected Leader's credibility is often the manifestation of people's emotional reactions to change. New leadership always frightens people. When the new leader is the Unexpected Leader, this escalates normal amounts of fear to near terror for those who struggle believing it is your turn to lead.

Establishing credibility requires you to sustain a high level of composure even when the emotions of change are hurtful or angering. Be very good in your new leadership position. Strive for excellence in both the technical and relational aspects of your work. In all due time, as you prove to non-believers you can get the job done, they will believe in you too.

PAYING IT FORWARD

Unexpected leaders are concerned about paying success forward to emerging "Unexpecteds." These leaders recognize their success or lack thereof will be used to gauge whether someone like them emerges as a leader again. Keep your eye on others in the organizations who demonstrate leadership ability that may not be seen. Take these people under your wing and mentor them. Do not forget where you came from. Make sure your legacy of leadership includes preparing the next generation of Unexpected Leaders to walk in your shoes.

We recognize how traditions of leadership prevent certain people from being seen as leadership material. We are committed to elevating this talent pool wherever we work. It is our hope the new energy and style of Unexpected Leaders adds value to the communities, organizations, and companies we serve.

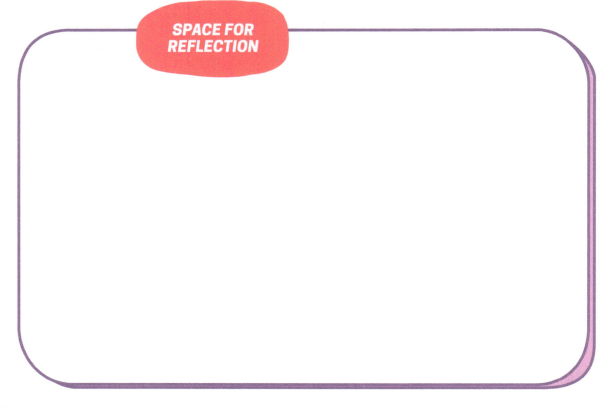

UNBOUGHT, UNBOSSED, UNDAUNTED

*DOES YOUR BUSINESS ACTIVITY
ALIGN WITH YOUR VALUES*

"Unbought. Unbossed." In 1972, the first African American Woman elected to the US Congress, Shirley Chisholm, proclaimed these words as her slogan for her presidential campaign. She was a politician, author, and educator, and undaunted in her quest for human rights. Her words strongly resonate with me today. This is the type of leadership needed if businesses are going to succeed today. The pressure of today's business environment places leaders in positions they have never been in before. Many question their abilities and are being pressed to work in ways they may not support or believe in. I observe many leaders under pressure become willing to compromise themselves and others on the journey to leadership success. This compromise almost always yields ethical dilemmas and negative outcomes for them and the businesses they represent.

In my work with leaders, I recognize it takes great courage to remain uncompromised in the face of business pressure. Leaders who do not bend on issues of principle or ethics often find themselves isolated, ridiculed, or even marginalized. However, in my work with these courageous leaders, they believe what they go through is worth it in the end. The primary goal for them is to only engage in business activity that aligns with their beliefs, principles, and values. They commit to being unbought, unbossed, and undaunted by what people think of them. When I discuss this concept with clients, they are very clear about what these words mean to them.

UNBOUGHT LEADERS

will not "sell out" their beliefs, principles, and values. This leader is skilled at making it clear what motivates them is doing "good and right" business at all times. Their deepest desire is to engage others in doing what is good for the business in the right way daily. These leaders refuse to let the influence of pressure or money sway them from this core principle.

UNBOSSED LEADERS

will not be bullied into doing anything they can't support. Bullying is not only an issue in public schools. Bullying also goes on in business environments — it just takes on a different look. Pressuring a leader to agree to a decision simply because a majority of others think it is the right thing to do is a form of bullying. Withholding funds from a leader's organization because they don't agree with a process or project is a form of bullying.

Suggesting a leader's reputation will be damaged if they don't get on board with what another group of leaders believes is right is a form of bullying. Mobilizing others to "blacklist" a leader because they just won't go with the flow is a form of bullying. This leader remains unbossed in the face of business bullying. This is the leader who calls out this activity and those doing it to point out how bullying in a business environment never adds value to the overall achievement of business goals.

These times try the souls of leaders. The business environment is volatile and changing all that most leaders once knew. The pressure could make it easy to compromise beliefs, principles, and values. Not every person is built to lead during this time. However, those that choose to do so will benefit from practicing the philosophies, skills, and behaviors of the unbought, unbossed, and undaunted leader.

UNDAUNTED LEADERS

are not held back to what others think of them. This leader knows who they are, what they believe, and what they will or will not do. What others think of them is not their business. Their business is to focus strategically on what they think of themselves. These leaders also actively develop and practice courage strategies, so fear does not prevent effective leadership. Today's business environment is filled with dynamics that create fear. Given this, they utilize an array of skills and techniques to engage employees in conversation about these dynamics to reduce fear and create strategies to address issues that are fear-producing.

REMEMBER YOU DESCEND FROM GREAT WOMEN.

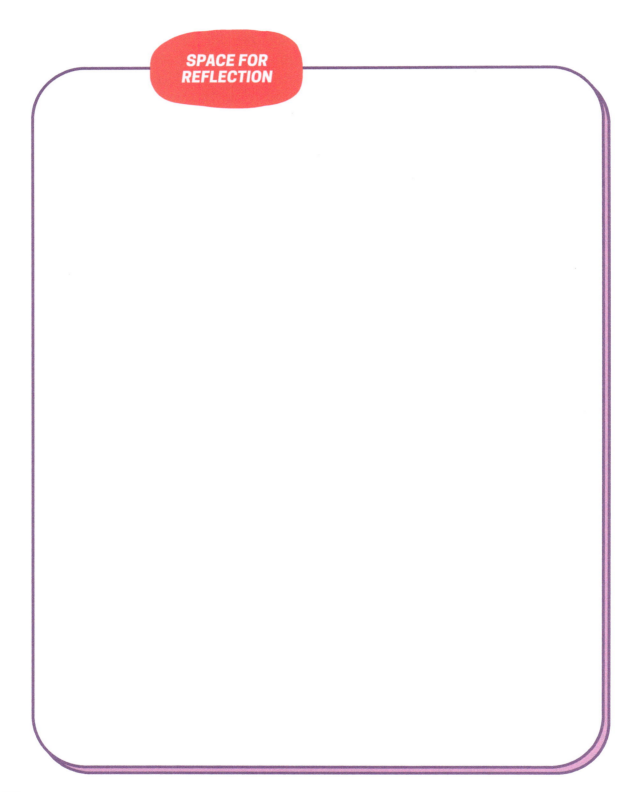

CREDIBILITY COUNTS

IS YOUR CREDIBILITY STRONG OR COMPROMISING?

Each day, I have the pleasure of observing factors that contribute to effective leadership, and I am paying deep attention to the concept of personal and professional credibility as a factor of effective leadership. Leaders must pay attention to whether or not they are experienced as credible by colleagues and employees. As I focus on studying the relationship between credibility and leadership, I notice many people willingly compromise themselves in this area. Leaders do not realize that compromised credibility has a direct impact on business results.

There are organizational factors that contribute to compromised leadership credibility. Dysfunctional company culture entices leaders to compromise credibility. Dysfunctional companies are filled with ineffective strategic leadership, ineffective operational managers, dissatisfied employees, and inconsistent business practices. When these factors are part of a company's culture, an atmosphere of survival of the fittest is created. People behave primarily in their own best interest. There is great concern about being thrown under the bus. This dynamic makes it easy for leaders to engage in behaviors that cause them to lose credibility with peers and employees.

Leaders often take credibility for granted. They seldom assess whether they are being experienced as a credible leader. I support a notion put forth by many leadership development experts: there is a direct connection between being credible and the ability to drive business results. I believe that being a trusted leader is a result of having credibility and building high trust relationships with colleagues and employees. Given this, it is important that leaders are intentional about having credibility with those they lead and manage.

ALIGNMENT OF WORDS AND DEEDS

Credibility and trust are interrelated. Leaders must always remember that they are always observed by staff, and people are looking to see if what you say translates into what you do. This continuity of words and behavior leads people to trust the leader and emulate their behavior.

ACHIEVING GOALS

By aligning your words and deeds, by paying attention to your actions, by always being aware that your credibility is at stake, will help you to drive the behaviors that lead to achieving goals. Success gets to be a habit like anything else you do.

All business achievement is directly tied to whether employees are willing to follow those leading them. Credibility, which is central to trust, plays a significant role in building relationships that inspire others to follow your lead. Take time to assess your personal and professional credibility. Enhance areas of strength but focus on improving the core weaknesses. Credibility really counts.

INFLUENCING OTHERS THROUGH MENTORING

INFLUENCING OTHERS CAN EFFECT THE FUTURE.

The philosophy that leadership is about one life influencing another is not always considered as one develops as a leader. When leaders embrace this philosophy great things almost always happen. One way to influence another's life is through mentoring. Pat Summit, the legendary women's basketball coach for Tennessee announced her retirement publicly on ESPN. She is one of my favorite leaders. In addition to being an amazing basketball technician, Pat Summit understands the powerful effect mentoring has on teams. During her coaching career, she made the connection between influencing the lives of young women by serving as a mentor and her capacity to turn these same young women into great basketball players. Clearly, this philosophy worked for her. She belongs to the elite group of coaches with numerous championships under their belts. Her stellar record indicates that mentoring can make a qualitative difference in one's desire to succeed and to influence others to succeed.

This same philosophy is being embraced by organizations and companies. I see a rise in the development of formal mentoring programs in every sector of business. These programs involve top leaders, including CEOs who agree to mentor strategically selected high potential employees.

Mentoring is a person-to-person relationship focused on the professional development of the mentee. The mentor oversees the career and development of the mentee through teaching, career counseling, providing psychological/emotional support, protecting and, at times, sponsoring the mentee for promotion in the organization or company. This definition speaks directly to strategies used to influence the life of the mentee. Mentors have direct influence on the mentee's career by providing this specific type of business-based support, caring and concern. Within effective mentoring relationships, the mentor and mentee:

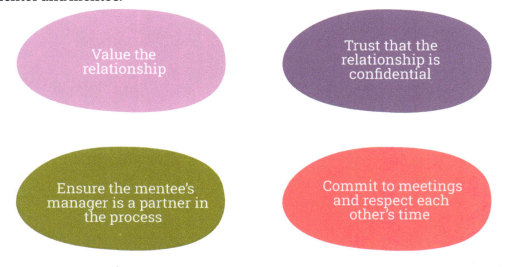

The development of a formal mentoring program must be strategic. Top leaders typically lay the foundation for program development by determining how mentoring aligns with business and workforce development goals. Human Resource professionals are empowered with time and financial support to organize teams to design the program. Selection criteria are developed to ensure leaders and employees are appropriate for participation in the mentoring program.

Evaluation mechanisms are in place to ensure mentor/mentee relationships deliver business results. It is easy to reduce mentoring to another "touchy/feely" workplace initiative. However, there are many documented business benefits that result from successfully implementing formal mentoring programs. Mentoring is a business strategy that contributes to the achievement of business goals.

Far too often leadership is reduced to titles, positions, flow charts, and day-to-day workplace tasks. Although each of these is an important aspect of leadership, leaders like Pat Summit frequently identify their greatest leadership success as having the opportunity to positively influence the life of another. This is one philosophy I encourage every leader to adopt. Consider being a mentor and/or developing a mentoring program in your organization or company.

Mentoring truly contributes to the achievement of business goals. Also, of equal importance, mentoring increases personal satisfaction and can enhance the entire leadership and employee experience.

LEGACY BUILDING: VISIONING EXERCISE

Directions:
Below is an imagined situation. Read the direction for each segment, and consider that your answers are the description for your legacy.

You are selected as one of the most effective leaders in your state. You attend an event where you and other leaders will be recognized. When you arrive, you notice there is a large press group to greet you. As you exit the car you overhear them commenting on specific attributes you have which have contributed to your selection for this award.

What specific attributes were mentioned about you that led to your success?

1

2

3

You arrive at the award ceremony, where you are called to deliver remarks. What do you want to make clear to the audience? (The following questions will inform your thinking.)

What three actions did you take to arrive at this success-point in your life?

1

2

3

In addition to motivating yourself, what other values helped you succeed?

1

2

3

You know that much of your success could not have happened without lots of support from mentors.

What did you learn from mentors that was significant to your success?

1

2

3

You want the audience to know how important you think it is to "pay it forward" to those you see as future leaders.

What are the three most important attributes you think they will need to succeed?

1

2

3

As you close your remarks, you want to leave the audience with a one-liner about what exactly it was that gave you the confidence, competence, courage, and calm to be the best leader you could be. What is this important one-liner, or personal motto?

EVERYDAY LEADERSHIP

HOW DO "EVERYDAY LEADERS" MAKE A DIFFERENCE IN BUSINESS COMMUNITIES, AND THE WORLD?

YOU CAN'T FAIL BECAUSE YOUR HISTORY SAYS YOU CAN'T

I frequently ponder this question as I work with leaders to develop the philosophies, behaviors, and skills used daily in the workplace. I believe it is everyday women and men who truly make the difference in our community, state, country, and world. Each day millions of people enter businesses, organizations, schools, churches, and homes pressured to be the leader who makes a difference. These "everyday leaders" use tenacity and persistence to ensure missions are advanced and goals are set. These everyday leaders make decisions that lead to improvements and innovations. These everyday leaders set a moral compass that inspires ethical behavior. These everyday leaders are people like you and me who truly change the world.

Many companies and organizations shove the newest leadership concept at their leaders hoping that this will somehow produce great results. This "flavor of the week" approach to leadership development is primarily an academic experience for everyday leaders. In our ongoing commitment to develop leaders, we must create spaces and places that allow leaders to tell the truth about leading in "real time." New leadership concepts in books can provide a context for leadership but the authors aren't in the workplace or community to support the translation of this reading into effective leadership action in the "trenches."

As I work with everyday leaders, I am learning what they most desire is an opportunity to be supported as they practice their profession. I've learned from them that leadership is not an exact science. Becoming an effective leader requires a willingness to step into a great experiment that is very dynamic. However, I notice those who find consistent congruence between values, beliefs, and actions create a rock-solid base from which great leadership grows.

Everyday leaders want to network with each other. They know the isolation of leading and need to hear best practices from colleagues.

Everyday leaders need an opportunity to process mistakes and challenges without being viewed as weak or incompetent.

Everyday leaders want to discuss work-life balance as an issue affecting both women and men and find solutions that allow them to be successful at work and home.

Everyday leaders think about their legacies and how to ensure that what they do today serves the success of those who will follow them in the future.

While new concepts in books or seminars can encourage thinking about leadership development, in the end everyday leaders are women and men who simply arrive each day trying to be their best as they grow in the profession of leadership. It is important to celebrate their contributions and to provide consistent ongoing support for their good works. Everything really does rise and fall on leadership, and we must ensure those who choose to lead in the community, state, country, and world know they are supported, respected, and honored for all they do each day. Onward and Upward leaders!

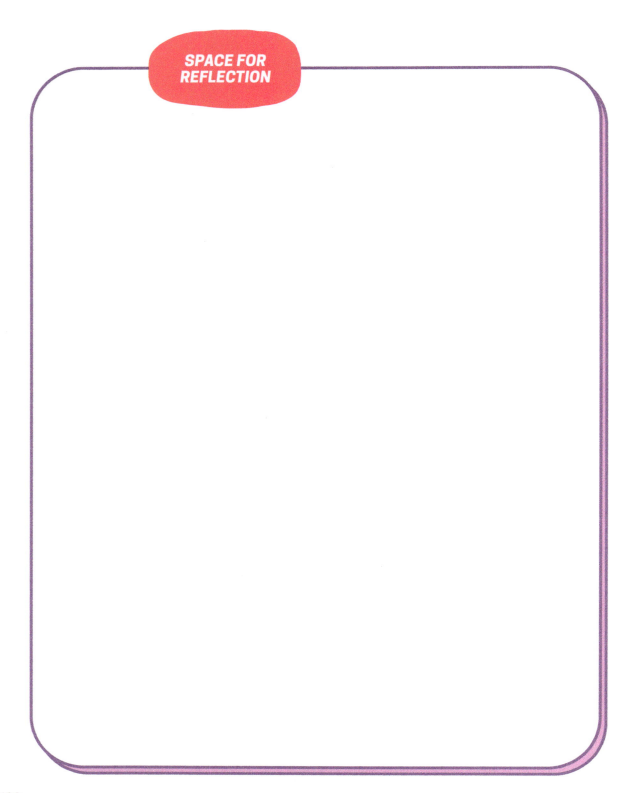

WORK HARD PLAY HARDER!

ARE YOU A LEADER WHO WORKS HARD BUT IGNORES SELF CARE?

I frequently speak on the topic of self-care. When I was speaking to more than 200 caregivers at the Alzheimer Association of Central New York conference, sharing my experiences as a caregiver, I realized I too needed to practice improvement in the area of self-care.

Confession-I am a recovering workaholic. I love my work and have no problems staying up all night to get it done. To me, there is great joy and challenge in being the President/CEO of a leadership development corporation. The joy-every day I support leaders in finding the way to authentic leadership. The challenge is every day I say something that causes me to reflect on how I support myself in my ongoing quest to be an authentic leader. However, I learned the hard way that ignoring self-care, engaging in all work with no play makes for a very sick and tired leader. One particular incident put me on the path to recovery.

My daughter was treated for cancer from 1995-2000. I was a new entrepreneur and there was a lot of buzz around the business I owned with my partner. I was the typical self-deluded Superwoman. In partnership with my husband, I took care of my daughter, her little brother, served clients, and continued to serve on several boards. I did some of my very best work during this challenging era for "Team Webber-McLeod." I was a skilled workaholic who proudly operated on 2-3 hours of sleep a night. But I never acknowledged the toll being a workaholic took on my life. Publicly I was on a professional roll, privately I was a hot mess and lied to myself about this daily. Does this scenario resonate with any of my sister and brother leaders out there?

I had the opportunity to meet with a therapist during this time. I needed help holding up amid pediatric cancer. She asked how I was doing. With the arrogance of a true workaholic, I told her how successful I was operating on 2-3 hours of sleep a night. She looked me square in the eye and said, "Gwen, do you think this is normal?" I was shocked. Why ask this question? Doesn't every successful leader operate without sleep? The scary part-I did think this was normal.

In that moment I realized that like me, far too many leaders are fueled by anxiety, fear, and exhaustion. Shortly after this conversation, I committed to fueling the balance of my career with rest, reflection, and rejuvenation. My primary professional goal is to be calm. To focus on this I adopted a mantra,

WORK HARD, PLAY HARDER

Being a workaholic is harmful to effective leadership. It causes rushed judgment, foggy memory, stressed relationships, and lackluster decision-making. None of these things contribute to effective leadership. I believe leaders need to play harder. I am so passionate about this that Gwen, Inc. executive coaching clients include leadership goals for self-care in their coaching plans.

Playing hard comes in the form of big and small activities. Take a ten-minute mental trip to the Bahamas. Give yourself the gift of wellness via massage or exercise. Meet friends for dinner, drinks, and dancing. Guess what? Leaders can and should take their full vacation time and work survives without you.

Today's leaders must engage in rest, reflection, and rejuvenation to keep pace with everything happening in their companies. They are successful only when they manage work in ways that leave time to work hard and play harder.

Are you a workaholic? If yes, I invite you to join me in recovery. Something amazing happens in the life of a leader when they are intentional about self-care. Open your calendar and schedule some playtime today.

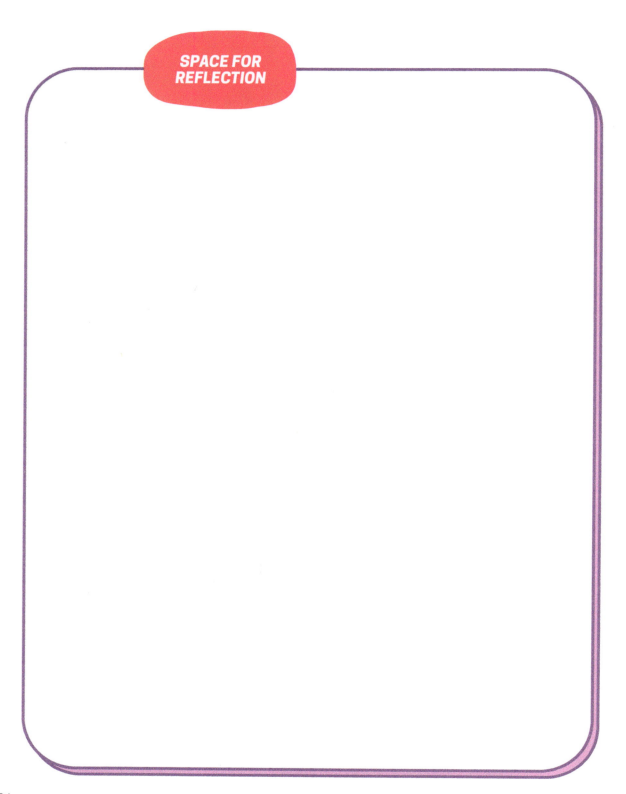

STAYING
ON TRACK

**ARE YOU SABOTAGING
YOUR OWN LEADERSHIP?**

The phone rings and I hear, "Hello Gwen, I think I might be fired today." I ask what may seem like an odd question, "Do you want to be fired?"

The leader responds, "What do you mean?" I ask, "Is it possible you are sub-consciously dissatisfied in this leadership position? Could you be engaged in behaviors that are derailing your leadership as a result?

The leader is quiet for a minute and acknowledges they have been dissatisfied in their position for some time, secretly longing for a new opportunity but afraid to leave. This conversation leads to a technical assistance meeting, helping them to decide if it is time for a graceful exit strategy or one that helps them get back on track.

This call exemplifies something I witness regularly in talented, dissatisfied leaders who engage in behaviors/factors that derail their leadership. A team of researchers at the Center for Creative Leadership in Greensboro North Carolina dissected factors that caused talented leaders to derail. Their findings inspired me to pay attention to this challenge with my clients. I ask leaders to consider why a leader consciously or sub-consciously engages in factors which cause underperformance that can derail them in their position. Dissatisfaction and fear of doing something about the situation is frequently mentioned as a cause for derailment. I observe a connection between dissatisfaction, poor performance, and leadership derailment in the following areas.

Dissatisfied leaders struggle with interpersonal skills in the workplace, forgetting relationships really matter. When leaders struggle with this it impacts the achievement of business outcomes. When outcomes are not achieved, leaders derail.

Effective leadership is a combination of philosophy, skill, and behaviors. Leaders often experience dissatisfaction when they feel "technically" irrelevant in the workplace. In today's business environment leaders can't use yesterday's skills to tackle today's complex problems. More and more I hear from leaders that they are concerned that skills that helped them win their current position are no longer appropriate.

They fear they can't perform successfully because of this professional reality. In particular, many discover they lack the skill of critical thinking which leads to the derailing factor of poor judgment. A leader must have the capacity to assess situations, think through decisions and determine the best course of action for the business to stay on track.

Leaders often feel overwhelmed by the need to collect and analyze data for strategy development and decision making. As many are not trained to do this, dissatisfaction in their performance results, leading to ill-designed strategies and decisions, causing leaders to derail.

Failure to develop high potential employees is another reason leaders derail. Most businesses operate under high stress, on day-to-day operations and neglect employee development. This causes dissatisfaction for the leader because although they know the importance of employee development, finding the time to do it is difficult. Successful leaders have a strong "bench" of high potential employees prepared to lead at any time. These individuals are strategically developed with the understanding that this investment in them is tied to a future with the business. When high potential employees believe a leader is not committed to their development they leave. Over time the loss of talent causes leaders to derail.

At some point, most leaders experience dissatisfaction in a position. It is important to pay attention to this dynamic because unattended these feelings lead to underperformance. Leaders must make the connection between dissatisfaction, poor performance, and derailing in their positions. If it is not time for a graceful exit, then make a conscious decision to get back on track. Remember Gwen, Inc.'s tag line—"leadership is not a job to do alone." Engage the support of a trusted peer or executive coach to assist in developing a specific plan to get back on track.

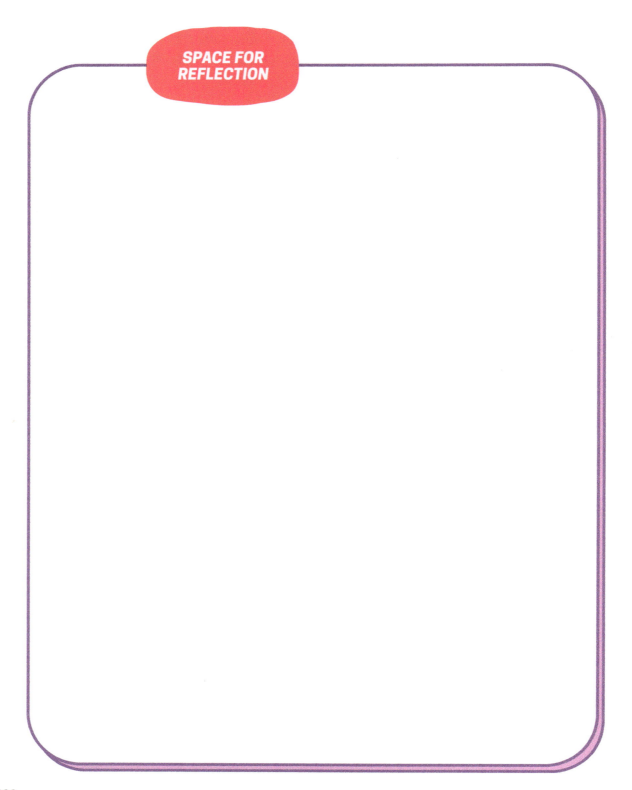

SPACE FOR REFLECTION

Inspirational Poem: Before you continue your learning, reflect for a moment on

MAY THE WORK I'VE DONE SPEAK FOR ME
- Sullivan Pugh (The Consolers, Sullivan and Iola Pugh)

May the works I've done speak for me.
May the works (I've done) speak for me.
When I'm resting in my grave,
There's nothing more to be said;
May the works (the works I've done)
Let it speak for me, (for me)

May the life I live speak for me.
May the life (I live) speak for me.
When I'm resting in my grave,
There's nothing more to be said;
May the works (the works I've done)
Let it speak for me, (for me).

The works I've done,
Sometimes it seems so small,
It seems like I've done nothing at all.
Lord I'm (Learning) and depending on you
If I do right you're gonna see me through;
May the works (the works I've done),
Let it speak for me, (for me)

Speak for me,
Speak for me

RESULTS OF LEARNING: SECTION THREE

Now that you have read the essays, completed your worksheets, considered the resource essays, and reflected on the inspiring words of The Consolers, think about how you will answer this question:

AS A RESULT OF YOUR LEARNING EXPERIENCE IN SECTION THREE, HOW WILL THIS KNOWLEDGE HELP ME BECOME THE LEADER I ASPIRE TO BE?

Take time to identify the answer to the question above, identifying at least one action you can take in your own leadership life as a direct result of completing Section Three. Also write down any concerns, situations, or questions which your reading has helped you identify. The writing space below provides you with an opportunity to collect all your thoughts in one place, which will be helpful later in completing your Personal Leadership Plan.

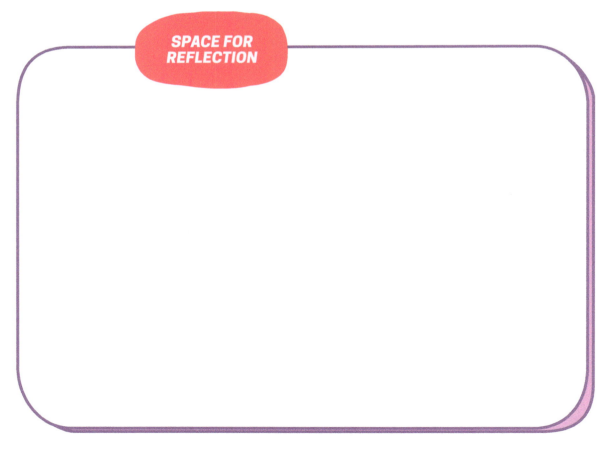

COMPILATION WORKSHEET:

Review the notes you have made from Sections 1-3 and compile them into one document for use in Section 4. You may notice trends or recurring themes and concerns. Organize them into groups or categories so you can find commonality.

SPACE FOR REFLECTION

INTRODUCTION TO SECTION FOUR

GOAL SETTING: CREATING PERSONAL LEADERSHIP DEVELOPMENT PLAN

Using the lessons learned about yourself and your journey through leadership development, from the first three sections of the book, you will create your Personal Leadership Plan below, a specific, workable guide you can refer to over and over, for the inspiration and skills to ensure your success. This plan will guide your decision making for 12 months, as you work toward becoming the leader you want to be. It will support your ongoing growth as a leader, helping you grow as a confident, competent, courageous, and calm leader.

There is power in writing down your plan. It enables you to move from where you are on your leadership path, to become the leader you aspire to be. As you envision the leader you want to be, you will now have a living tool for support as you create your authentic leadership self.

As you begin to work on your plan, keep these points in mind:

 You are creating a comprehensive picture of your leadership strategy.

 It clarifies how your personal and professional efforts are connected to ensure you achieve the best outcomes at work and at home.

 It includes meaningful target measures and a sequence of activities that help you focus on what is most important to you.

 If you have more than one leadership development goal, create a 12-month plan for each, so you can concentrate on specifics.

REVIEWING YOUR KNOWLEDGE:

As a preliminary step to creating your plan on the next pages, take some time to review the core knowledge you have gained from Sections 1-3. This will help you inform your answers to the Personal Leadership Plan questions.

1 Review your own compiled notes from the book, found at the end of Section 3, looking for significant commonalties you have identified:

2 Transfer your **Personal Mission Statement** from Section 1 below. It will help you stay on track as you work through the plan development. Remember it is your foundation for your personal and professional life, a guiding light, and anchor of clarity that keeps you true to yourself.

144

3 Thinking about the lessons and skills you learned in Section 2, identify specific areas you feel need work to help you attain your leadership goals:

4 Thinking about the **Visioning Exercise** in Section 3, what is the impact you want your leadership to have on work and home?

5 What are your deeply held enduring beliefs that define what you stand for and how you practice your leadership?

6 How could your leadership legacy make a difference?

CREATING A PERSONAL LEADERSHIP PLAN WORKSHEET:

Directions:
Answer the questions below to create your own Personal Leadership Plan.

Each question may have single or multiple answers, depending on your career goal. Be as specific as possible in your answers.

When you have completed Questions 1-9, you will have the workable guide to your leadership success, supporting your ongoing growth as a leader.

THROUGHOUT THE BOOK WE QUOTE EXAMPLES OF INSPIRATIONAL WORDS FROM DIVERSE LEADERS. START YOUR PLAN BY ADDING A QUOTE YOU FEEL INSPIRES YOU TO NEW HEIGHTS.

1. **Your personal inspirational quote:**

2. **What is your leadership vision?** (*What do you hope will be different as a result of your leadership?*) Example: People feel empowered. They know their voices will be heard. My team achieves goals.

3. **What are your leadership values?** "I believe..."

4. Identify four strategic priorities for your leadership: what are these high-level actions you must take to be the leader you desire to be? Example: become a more effective communicator; improve professional skills, etc.

6. Identify actions you are willing to take to improve your leadership to reach this goal. Example: Set aside time each week for reading, network with other women leaders.

7. Who are the people who can help you achieve this goal, and why?
Example: My manager, mentors, and friends who are also aspiring leaders.

5. What is your leadership development goal? Example: To be more confident as a leader in my company, to position myself for promotion.

8. **What resources do you need to achieve the goal?** Example: certification in xyz skill, executive coaching, professional development.

9. What could hinder your progress? Example: not making time, low self-confidence, distractions from personal relationships.

10. Who can support you as work toward your goal? Example: My manager, mentors, friends, family an executive coach.

11. Commit to a start date, and forecast an end date

A FINAL THOUGHT FROM GWEN WEBBER-MCLEOD

Congratulations!
You completed *Your Leadership Journey: Living and Leading "In and On Purpose"*! I wrote this book to help women leaders recognize that the journey to leadership is an ever-evolving process. I hope one thing you learned about yourself gives you the confidence, competence, courage, and calm to be the leader you desire, or feel called to be. There is nothing greater than navigating the leadership journey living your wildest dreams doing work that aligns with your passion and purpose. As you position to activate your leadership plan, I want to remind you of an inspiration I shared at the beginning of your journey through this book:

Remember, leadership is a way of life and what you work on here is relevant to all aspects of life. It is my hope the experience you have as a result of reading this book helps you live and lead "in and on purpose." Press on sister leader! There is someone out there waiting for you to do the thing you've been called to do! That someone is you.

Onward and Upward!
Gwen

Gwen Webber-McLeod is inspired by these books on leadership. She encourages you to read them too.

GENERAL LEADERSHIP:

Developing the Leader Within You, John C. Maxwell
5 Levels of Leadership, John C. Maxwell
The Speed of Trust, Stephen M.R. Covey
The Five Dysfunctions of a Team, Patrick Lencioni
Good is Not Enough and Other Unwritten Rules for Minority Professionals, Keith R. Wyche

WOMEN'S LEADERSHIP:

Becoming, Michelle Obama
Dare to Lead, Brene Brown
When and Where I Enter, Paula Giddings
Lean In, Sheryl Sandberg
But Some of Us Are Brave, Patricia Bell-Scott
The Little Black Book of Success, Elaine Brown, Marsha Haygood, Rhonda McLean

INSPIRATIONAL:

Acts of Faith: Daily Meditations for People of Color, Iyanla Vanzant
Peace from Broken Pieces: How to Get Through What You're Going Through, Iyanla Vanzant
A Return To Love: Reflections on the Principles of A Course in Miracles, Marianne Williamson
The Confident Woman: Start Today Living Boldly and Without Fear, Joyce Meyer
Favorite Scripture from the Bible: Philippians 4:13; Joshua 1:9; Proverbs 1:3

GWEN WEBER-MCLEOD BIOGRAPHY:

Gwendolyn (Gwen) Webber-McLeod, M.S., is President/CEO of Gwen, Inc. She has over 30 years' experience in leadership/organization development, facilitation, strategic planning, the development of effective coalitions/collaborations, helping companies develop strategies for taking diversity and inclusion initiatives to the next level **(Diversity 2.0©)** and the strategic development of women and minority leaders breaking glass/cement ceilings in companies **(Unexpected Leaders®)**. Gwen is a frequently sought-after lecturer and conference keynote speaker on the topic of leadership. Her clients are CEOs, executive and mid-level managers, and leadership teams in public, private, health care and education businesses and organizations. **Gwen, Inc. exists for the sole purpose of helping leaders achieve business goals by focusing on the competencies of confidence, competence, courage, and calm.**

In 2009, Gwen founded the **You Can't Fail** (Because Your History Says You Can't) conference as an unforgettable, one of a kind, conference designed to provide a strategically designed multicultural leadership development experience for professional women of color and women leaders of other races and cultures who support them. It was founded as a way to pay her success forward to other women leaders. You Can't Fail is a unique opportunity to promote the positive growth of this important group of established and emerging leaders. In 2015 You Can't Fail was incorporated as a 501 (c) 3 charitable organization. You Can't Fail, Inc. is devoted to the development of the next generation of emerging women leaders of color.

Gwen is a published author with contributions most recently featured in *Resilience: Living Life by Design* by Dr. Deana Murphy published in 2015 and available on Amazon. Gwen's chapter **Thriving Through a Season of Grief** chronicles how the vision for incorporating Gwen, Inc. was the result of thriving through a difficult moment in life.

Gwen contributes her success to the support of her loving family and to working daily to simply be the type of leader she believes God called her to be — **A Servant Leader**.

Gwen has been Director of Communications for Wells College; Communications/ Development Director of the Seven Lakes Girl Scout Council; Executive Director of the National Women's Hall of Fame in Seneca Falls; Executive Director of the Booker T. Washington Community Center in Auburn, and Coordinator of Human Services for the Cayuga/Seneca Community Action Agency.

Gwen is a recognized leader who has a very active civic life. She takes great pride in serving on boards of directors that enhance and improve the lives of people at the local, state, and national level. Currently she is very excited to serve as the Co-chair of the WISE Women's Business Center where she acts on her interest in helping women entrepreneurs.

GWEN HAS FORMERLY SERVED ON THE BOARDS OF OR BEEN AFFILIATED WITH:

-Planned Parenthood of the Rochester and Syracuse Region Board Chair

-Member of Loretto in Syracuse New York Board of Directors

-The Central New York Women's Fund Chair Marketing Committee

-National Co-chair of the Planned Parenthood Federation of America's Social Marketing Advisory Resource Team.

-Past Board Chair and Interim CEO of the Cayuga County Chamber of Commerce, where she led efforts to refocus and reenergize the work and reputation of the Chamber in the community.

-Founding Board Member, Friends of Women's Rights National Park; Designed *Elizabeth and Me* program for middle school and high school girls based on the life of Elizabeth Cady Stanton, founder of the First Woman's Rights Convention in Seneca Falls, NY.

-Founding Board Member, past President, life-long advisor, You Can't Fail Inc., a charitable organization devoted to the development of the next generation of emerging women leaders of color and those who support them.

-Trustee of Cayuga Community College.

-The Central New York Business Council First Niagara Bank.

-Team advisor to the CNY Health Fellows teams, a project of the Community Health Foundation of Western and Central New York.

-Board chair of Booker T. Washington Community Center.

GWEN HAS RECEIVED MANY AWARDS DURING HER CAREER, INCLUDING:

-Auburn Cayuga NAACP Outstanding Community Service Award (1985)

-Central New York NOW Chapter Unsung Heroine Award (1990)

-Potsdam College added her name to the State University of New York Confederation Honor Roll (1991)

-The New York State Governor's Award for African Americans of Distinction. (1994)

-The Marjorie Dowdell Fortitude Award, presented to outstanding African American women by the Syracuse Chapter of Delta Sigma Theta Sorority. (1994)

-The Seven Lakes Girl Scout Council Woman of Excellence Award (1995)

-The Cayuga County Chamber of Commerce Board Chairs Award (2002)

-The New York State Senate Woman of Distinction Award from Senator Michael Nozzolio. Gwen's mother, the Honorable Barbara N. Webber, retired Jefferson County, New York legislator, also received this award, making them the first mother and daughter ever to receive the Woman of Distinction honor in the same year. (2004)

-Honored as one of CNY Business Journal's 20 Women in Business Honorees and received the Phyllis Goldman Encouragement Award for Women from the Cayuga County Chamber of Commerce. (2007)

-Elected to the Academy of Diversity Achievers, an award presented to successful diversity champions presented by the YWCA Syracuse and Onondaga County. (2008)

-Initiated into the Syracuse Alumnae Chapter of Delta Sigma Theta Sorority, a historic nationally renowned public service sorority for African American women. (Spring 2009)

-January 2010 Gwen received MLK Millennium Award from Cayuga County Branch of NAACP.

-Women Igniting the Spirit of Entrepreneurship "Faces of Success" award for being an outstanding woman entrepreneur and the Syracuse Zonta Foundation Crystal Award given to women whose work improves the status of girls and women. (Spring 2014)

-Recognized for Distinguished Service by the Syracuse Onondaga County NAACP (2016)

-Successful Business Women Award Mentor of the Year (2018)

-Inducted into the Auburn Cayuga NAACP Hall of Fame as a President and for her life-long commitment to social justice activism. (2019)

In 2019, Gwen accepted a nomination from the Cayuga County Democratic Party to be a candidate for the 14th district seat in the Cayuga County Legislature. Her nomination made her the first African American woman in the 226-year history of Cayuga County to run for the legislature. She lost by a narrow margin and her race made a significant impact on aspiring women politicians She follows in the footsteps of her parents Charles and Barbara Webber who made history by becoming the first African Americans elected to the Jefferson County Legislature in Watertown, NY.